Stories from my Younger Days

A Memoir

By

Lawrence E. Schmidt

STRATO SNOB PRESS

Lebanon   Paris   London

This book available from: www.createspace.com/3343817

ISBN 978-1-4382-2885-3

Cover: 34th Photo-Reconnaissance Squadron pilots, Wallace Bosworth (#624, on back cover), Neil Walters (#112) and Lawrence Schmidt (#235). Photo taken by Jack Quinn, August 19, 1944, near Chateaudun, France.

Back cover photos: Lawrence E. Schmidt, as a boy scout (1934), in the cockpit of his P-38 at Chalgrove field (1944) and at the Tillamook Oregon Air Museum (1997).

Photographs are property of Lawrence E. Schmidt except as noted in photo descriptions.

Strato Snob Press
33030 Tennessee Rd
Lebanon, OR 97355

*To Shirley, my dear wife and
"co-pilot" these past 61 years, and*

*To my fellow members of the
34th Photographic Reconnaissance
Squadron, heroes all.*

Contents

INTRODUCTION

Lawrence Schmidt wrote these stories when he was in his seventies. Equipped with a personal computer, his very first, and a good memory, he typed the stories, printed them on his home printer and gave copies to his children and grandchildren.

He gave me a copy of his "War Memories" in 1998 and "Growing up in Lebanon" in 2000. When I received my copies, I quickly scanned through them and filed them away. I was too preoccupied with a job and kids in college during those years to give the stories a careful reading.

Earlier this year, though, as we planned for an extended Schmidt Family Reunion, I remembered the stories and decided to reread them. This time, I finally realized what treasures they were, particular today, fifty, sixty, seventy years after the facts. They tell of times before automobiles and video became common, of how his family coped with the economic setbacks of the Depression, of the thrill of flying the fastest production airplane of its era, and of the unpredictable fortunes of war. In short, they recount and share experiences few of us can know today.

Dad produced the original copies on letter-sized paper, single-spaced in small fonts. They were fairly informal, more like a rough draft than a final draft. For the sake of preservation I felt they deserved better, so I decided to edit and collect them into this book.

In discussing this idea with my sister, Lisa, she mentioned yet another story that I had never seen, one Dad had written but not distributed. She had discovered it in his computer room and saved a copy. That story, "Picking Hops in Buena Vista," describes his experience picking hops near Salem, Oregon during the 1930s. It is also included in this book. Since his "War Memories" story was lengthy, I took the liberty of reorganizing it into three, separate, shorter stories, each covering one year in his Army Air Corps service. Otherwise, I edited sparingly, trying to keep them in Dad's voice.

We are fortunate that he took the time to write these stories down. Thank you, Dad!

Mark Schmidt
Welches, Oregon
May 15, 2008

1922 TO 1940
Growing up in Lebanon

Lebanon, The Town

The first pioneers came to the Lebanon area in 1846, a little over 150 years ago. I am now 77 as I write this story in 2000. I was born on November 1, 1922. To me, it is interesting that I have lived throughout the last half of the white man's recorded history in this area.

When pioneers settled this Willamette Valley, which is some of the best farmland in the world, they cleared the land for farming by falling the large Douglas Firs that were here. They split a lot of the timber into rails and fenced their homesteads with the traditional zigzag rail fences. The sawmills followed soon after the first settlers, so it wasn't long before the resulting lumber was turned into houses and barns.

In 1922, Lebanon's business buildings were constructed out of the same lumber. The town was built entirely of wood, vertical board and batten design, until the Masonic Lodge was constructed in 1884 at the corner of Main and Sherman streets.

The older buildings in Lebanon are all gone now and the huge barns, some which were picturesque, are also gone. So are the rail fences and the stately trees that once graced Lebanon's school campuses. But in 1922, the year of my birth into the shoemaker's family that had emigrated from Leofeld, Saskatchewan in 1920, most of those pioneer structures were still in place. There was split rail fencing by the mile in every direction. The beautiful old barns were intact and in use. Over half of downtown Lebanon's wooden buildings were still being used.

The town setting was compact. The town's homes were constructed around the central business area. The 1,890 inhabitants at that time all lived within easy walking distance of the town center and each other. The downtown area was about one half-mile square. There were some small farms near the city's outskirts, and larger farms scattered over the valley between the other towns.

Businesses in town were open from 7:00 a.m. to 7:00 p.m. during the week, but from 7:00 a.m. to 10:00 p.m. on Saturday. Everyone came to town on Saturday afternoons and stayed until the businesses closed that night. The farm ladies brought excess cream and eggs to town. They sold the cream to Bohles Creamery and the eggs to the grocery store. They did their grocery shopping for the next week, caught up on the local news and gossip, visited JC Penneys for cloth and thread, and shopped various other stores for their needs.

My family, in front of our '24 Dodge, summer, 1926. I am the small one, front row, right.

The farm men would visit the town's hardware and blacksmith shops to get what they needed and talk "shop" with other farmers. The loggers came in from the Lacomb area, which was east of Lebanon about ten miles in the Cascade foothills. Their interests were a little different. After dropping off their logging boots at the shoe shop to install new sharp points (called corks and used to give them traction on the slippery logs and terrain) on the bottom of their boots, the loggers would go to one of the town's two pool halls to play pool and drink beer.

The pool halls were lively places. Any male of any age could go in and watch the grown-ups play pool, snooker or billiards. There was always a huge wood stove burning brightly and lots of benches for people to sit and watch. In the wintertime the only places to keep warm were the pool halls and the Lebanon Hotel lobby. The hotel was across the street from the Kuhn movie theater. Movies were a great source of entertainment for everyone. The movies changed three times a week. On Saturday and Sunday, the shows ran continuously from 2:00 p.m. till midnight.

The younger people amused themselves playing games, going to the movies, or just standing around on the street corners and talking to one another. As most of the kids were in town with their parents, there was always a lot going on. The downtown area was always full of people, especially on Saturday night. Everyone enjoyed coming to town to socialize and meet friends. There was a camaraderie and closeness in the small community that was a source of great pleasure to all of us.

Cars were nice, but they took away the personal touch and spontaneity of these weekly gatherings. As people began taking to their cars for every trip to town, parking soon became a problem. There was a lot of congestion in town, but not the same conversation or leisure activities as before. The small independent stores run by one or two local people and catering to limited needs gradually gave way to the large, impersonal megastores we have today. No longer needing to go to one place for meat, another for thread and sundries, another for bakery goods, people gradually lost the feeling of neighborliness so evident in small towns of that time.

The Schmidt Farm

We lived in a house on North Williams Street at the time of my birth. Our family at that time consisted of my mother Marie Ann (39), my father Nicholas (46), my brothers, Peter (18), Nicholas Jr. (12), and Leo (5), and sisters, Agnes (16), Catherine (or Corky, 14), Grace (7), Isabell (3), and Mary (2). I have one younger brother, Norman, who was born when I was five. I also had four siblings who died very young.

I remember little of the house on Williams Street. I recall a manual sewing machine setting on the back of the house that we used to pedal furiously. A mental picture of my mother washing my face as I sat on the rail of the back porch is the only other memory from that house and that time.

In 1926, when I was three, my father purchased a ten-acre farm complete with a small barn, chicken coop, hog pen and sundry other buildings, such as a tiny smoke house. The farm was situated one mile south of Lebanon's city limits, which at that time extended south to Milton Street. The farm had a two-acre prune orchard and a three-acre pasture north of the barn (now occupied by the back of the Safeway store on South Main Street). Four acres were planted in wheat and the remaining acre was reserved for the house and other farm buildings.

It turned out to be an excellent buy as the Depression arrived three years later. My father had homesteaded in Canada with his parents, so he had a complete knowledge of animal husbandry, farming and generally making a living without outside help. With his shoe shop downtown and the small farm, we weathered the Depression nicely. We had little money, but our table was always full of good food.

Grade School

In September 1928, not quite six years old, I started the first grade. At that time, the Lebanon elementary school was on South Second Street near the canal. This was an old school. It had a large front porch with a cupola high over head. It was a two-story building with a full basement. There was a large fire escape slide in the rear of the building, extending from the second story to the ground. It was supposed to be used exclusively for fire drills, but it got more use than that.

I walked to school in the morning with my sisters, Mary, Isabell, and Grace, and my brother, Leo. We walked down River Road (now called Russell Drive) to

Main Street (Highway 20), then turned north on Main Street, continuing past two houses and a fox farm near the south canal bridge (site of the present day Shop and Kart grocery store).

After crossing the canal bridge, we were soon under the canopy of eight enormous maple trees. These trees paralleled Main for two blocks. They were so large, their branches extended completely over both lanes of traffic. Truly a distinguished entrance to our little town. These trees were destroyed when they turned the two-lane Main Street into a four-lane road in 1947.

After crossing the south canal bridge we would cut across open fields to Second Street and on to school. I don't remember too much from First Grade. One thing I do remember, though, was the time I waited in the basement until the janitor came to lock up the school.

I got out of class at 2:30 p.m., so it was my custom to wait in the basement until my sisters were dismissed at 3:30. Then we would walk home together. One day they forgot about me; I just kept waiting for

My mom and me, 1928.

them. When the janitor made his rounds to lock all the school doors, he discovered me waiting in the basement.

[9]

So I started to walk home by myself. By this time it was 4:30 and my mother had already organized a search for me. We met under the big maple trees on South Main and returned home safe and happy. After a few weeks my mother let me walk home with other first graders who lived out our way.

Our farmhouse didn't have electricity, so we kept two kerosene lamps lit at night. One was always in the front room and the other was carried from the kitchen to the dining room as it was needed. As soon as dinner was over and the dishes washed, we would gather around the dining room table to do homework. There were no distractions in those days, so I kind of liked doing the homework.

I learned to read at an early age and was an avid reader of both fiction and non-fiction. At that time the Lebanon library was full of World War I adventure novels. There was a complete set of Horatio Alger books, along with the Tom Swift series about scouting and college. I read a lot about the explorers' trips to the poles, Charles Lindbergh, Lawrence of Arabia, and the settling of the West. There were stories of 19th century Indian fighters, the events along the Oregon Trail, the adventures of Buffalo Bill Cody and other happenings.

To me the city library was a gold mine and I couldn't wait to mine it. I have continued my love of reading and learning and it is still one of my favorite pastimes.

In 1929, when I was in the second grade, we were given a six-week school holiday. We were moving to a new school, Queen Anne School. We were happy with this vacation, but didn't know they would extend the school year to make up for the lost time. The new school held all of the grade school children in Lebanon at that time. It had eight classrooms, an office, and a large gym with a gravel floor. Queen Anne was only a half-mile from our farm, an easy walk.

I completed my grade school years at Queen Anne. All the students got to know each other well. Folks didn't move much in that era, so the faces at school were always familiar. School came easy for me, though I wasn't always on my best behavior. Many times I was reprimanded for wisecracking or inattentiveness. Still, I enjoyed going to school and always looked forward to going back after summer vacation.

In the springtime, the kids went to school barefoot as soon as their parents would let them. The boys thought it was cool to be the first to go barefoot in the spring. I was usually the first one. I walked to school along the railroad track after the fourth grade, so I would take off my shoes and socks and stash them under the railroad bridge and put them back on during the walk home. This allowed me to be the first barefoot kid in school, about 30 days before my parents thought it warm enough to leave the shoes at home.

We went barefoot all summer except for going to Mass on Sundays. Most kids did the same thing, though sometimes it got me into trouble. The worst incident of going barefoot cost me two months of my summer due to an injury.

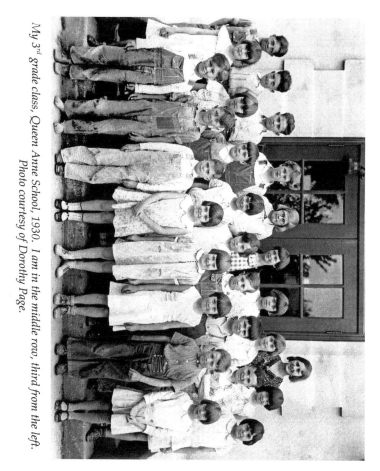

My 3ʳᵈ grade class, Queen Anne School, 1930. I am in the middle row, third from the left. Photo courtesy of Dorothy Page.

Our Home

The water supply for our house was a large, hand pump, standing four feet high on one side of the kitchen. There was no sink in the kitchen. When you raised that handle and came down with it, the water went into a large trough on the kitchen floor, unless you placed a container there to catch the water. The trough drained to the outside. The drain continued under the driveway and over to a field next to the house. This was the extent of our plumbing. One good feature of this pump was a large valve on the pump's base, which diverted water into the livestock water trough in the barnyard. I am sure you can guess who was responsible for keeping it full.

Our house only had three bedrooms, so my dad converted the cellar, at the back of the house, into a fourth bedroom. He did this by digging the cellar floor four feet deeper. Then over the cellar, he installed a floor, three foot above the level of the house floor. We then had the extra bedroom and a better cellar, too.

Dad never got around to improving the above ground part, the converted bedroom, so it was a lot colder than the rest of the house. Of course, we boys slept there. At night I could look out through the cracks in the wall and watch stars. There wasn't any heat, but we had down comforters, so we never slept cold.

The window my dad installed in one wall of the new bedroom must have come from his shoe shop, because it had a large advertising decal running diagonally across it, advertising in bold, black letters on a yellow background, the words "Seiberling Heels." No one ever bothered to scrape it off and it was still there when we sold the farm in 1936.

Farm Life

We had quite a lot of livestock on this small farm. This translated into work, which was apportioned among us children. The girls worked in the house and we boys did outside work, taking care of livestock and cleaning out the farm buildings every day.

We kept about a hundred chickens in a large coop. Half of them were White Leghorns and half were Rhode Island Reds. There were also two or three mean looking roosters in the pen, which intimidated me when I was very young. We had many bantam chickens, too, but they were small and ran wild. It was always amusing to see them with their little brood of chicks following the hens around.

Most of the time we kept two cows, but sometimes three. They had to be milked morning and night. I was seven when I started to help Leo with milking. First, we would go to the pasture, round them up and head them to the barn. Once they were in the stalls we would lock them in and throw some hay and feed down from the hayloft. There was a hole in the loft floor over their manger so this eased the labor of feeding them. You had to be careful when the loft was full of hay. If you weren't, you could slide on down into the manger with the hay.

One cow had a bad habit of lifting up her right hoof and setting it down inside the pail. She invariably waited until the pail was over half full to do this so she ruined a lot of milk. My dad solved this problem by getting a pair of "kickers" for her. They looked like handcuffs, but were open on one side so you could slide them over her ankles. She didn't like them and never lost time letting us know it, but she never put her hoof in the pail again.

We always had four or five cats around. They liked to gather in the barn at milking time to get their share of milk. The cats loved warm milk. We would put some in their dishes, but before we did that we would aim one of the cow's teats at a cat's mouth and let her fly. We didn't always hit their mouths, but if you got it on their faces they were satisfied. They licked it off with alacrity.

The milking chores were okay when Leo worked with me, but many times I milked alone. This wasn't too bad in the summer, but in the dark of winter, it got kind of spooky with the one small lantern for illumination. It seemed as if the shadows got darker and deeper the longer I stayed out in the barn. I always hurried as much as I could, but it still took about 45 minutes to milk two cows.

It is amazing how much milk a fresh cow has in her udder. We were getting two gallons a day from each of them. My mother would put it in large crocks in the pantry. When the cream rose to the top, she would skim off the cream, put it in the butter churn, and agitate it until some of it turned into butter. Then, when a little salt was added to it, you had some of the best butter you'd ever taste. Every night when we came home from school, we got a large slice of freshly baked bread with fresh butter on it. I can still smell the aroma from it.

Gardening and Filling the Pantry

My dad planted a large garden every spring. We raised enough vegetables to feed the livestock, besides what we needed for ourselves. The cultivation of this garden was left to Leo and myself. I was too short to reach the handles of the hand cultivator, so I ended up being the plough "horse." We attached a rope above the cultivator tines and the harness around my waist. I then pulled the cultivator up one row and down the other.

In the spring, we would fertilize the garden from the manure pile that grew outside the barn throughout the winter. This was the same manure pile I had dug a large hole in a few years earlier, when I was five.

My dad in his garden, ca. 1940.

When my brother, Norm, was born, being inquisitive I asked my mother where Norm had come from. She informed me he had come from the manure pile. Later, when I didn't show up for supper, they started looking for me. They found me digging furiously in the manure pile looking for another baby brother.

Carrying cow manure from the barn to the garden was not easy. The wheel on the wheelbarrow was made of steel, about an inch wide. With a load piled high, the wheel sank so deeply into the soft spring ground that you couldn't push it. So we "paved" the path between the barn and the garden with some flat boards to support the narrow wheel. This was fine unless you ran off the board, buried the wheel and ended up with the manure back on the ground. The distance from the barn to the garden was 100 yards, so manure hauling consumed a lot of time.

The resulting soil made for a good garden and also for some vigorous weed growth. The weed pulling chores went to my sisters, Mary and Isabell. I am sure they loved it as much as Leo and I loved our chores.

After the harvest came the canning. I got out of most of this, being otherwise busy. But I

Norm at the farmhouse, 1933.

remember all of us sitting around a large washtub, shelling peas. We filled that tub full of those little devils. Home-canned peas sure tasted good that following winter.

In the fall, my dad would butcher a young steer and two or more pigs that we had raised. My mother and older sisters, Grace and Catherine, would then can a lot of that meat. They cooked it before canning. The pork was salted down and put into wooden casks. We never wasted any of the animals. Dad made sausage by turning the intestines inside out and stuffing them with ground up meat, spices and herbs. These were then boiled and stored for the winter.

We made a large barrel of sauerkraut from the cabbage we grew. Grace and Catherine took care of all the vegetables, most of which were dug up in the fall and stored in our root cellar. Except for the prunes, we didn't have any fruit trees on our farm, so we had to go out for fruit. Fortunately, people always need shoes repaired, so my dad would trade shoe repair for apples, cherries and peaches.

We got apples at a farm just south of the dam on the Santiam River. We would take the back seat out of our 1924 Dodge touring sedan and fill it with apples. My dad drove through the orchard under the trees as we threw them in. People nowadays think the SUV's are something new, but our 1924 Dodge was used for everything, from a pick-up to a Sunday afternoon touring car.

We picked the cherries on shares, keeping half of what we picked. There were seven of us picking, so one evening's work would provide all the cherries we needed. We acquired the other fruits as well from various barters and share picking.

Come the middle of September, when school started, we had a pantry and a cellar full of quality food. Plus, we always had fresh milk and cheese and our mother baked three loaves of bread everyday. All this fed us in grand style all winter long. On Saturday nights, we went to town to buy staples, such as salt, sugar and flour. The total weekly grocery bill averaged only four dollars!

Swimming Fun

Although this labor occupied a lot of time, we were allowed to go swimming every afternoon after 1:00. As soon as I reached the age of seven, I was included in the daily walk to the city swimming pool. The swimming pool was located just off Wheeler Street in northeast

Lebanon, in the canal that passed through town. The official name was the Pacific Power Canal, but we called it the "Albany ditch." It was dug in the 1880's for barge traffic, but by the 1920s it was used only for Lebanon and Albany drinking water.

When they dug the canal, they had to install a small, wooden dam to retain the water in northeast Lebanon, near Wheeler Street. There was a low area there and a wooden dam was constructed to prevent the water from flowing into the low area and keep it moving on to Albany. The wooden dam became unusable after 30 years or so, and a concrete dam replaced it about 100 yards off from the canal. Construction of this new dam created a finger or bay jutting off from the canal channel. The bay was about 200 feet long and about the same depth as the canal. This was a large pool, with the canal running along the south, the new dam to the north, and willows on the west bank. The east bank was open and level, around three feet above the water. This is where our thoughtful city fathers constructed the town swimming pool.

It was an ideal place for swimming, about 10 feet deep in the middle and shallowing to six inches near the east bank. The shallower portion was fenced off with red buoys to form a wading pool and a small swimming area for beginners. In the middle of the pool there was a diving raft with a low and a high diving board. The low board was four feet above the water and the high one twelve feet. The raft with the diving boards was large enough for sunbathing and other playful pursuits.

The wooden dam had not completely rotted away so there was a slight current flowing from the canal into the pool, past the diving platform. If you followed the old dam, you could wade out to within 30 feet of the diving platform. As I mentioned earlier, there was a slight current in this area, so wading could be a little tricky for the younger ones. Of course the lifeguards knew this and kept a watchful eye for anybody who couldn't make it to the raft. As soon as we could, anyone who thought he could make it to the raft, tried to. I was rescued twice before I could make it to the raft.

During July the Red Cross gave swimming lessons for all levels, including Junior and Advanced Lifeguard. By the time I was 12, I had earned the Junior Lifeguard Badge. It was a triangular one with a lifeguard logo on it. I was proud of it and had my mother sew it on my new swimming trunks.

I had a good time at the old swimming hole. We went every day at one o'clock. It took 45 minutes to walk the two miles to the pool. So we had four hours of swimming before we would walk back to town to my father's shoe shop on Main Street and drive home with him at 6:00 p.m.

The raft's high dive platform was around ten feet square, with safety railing around it except for the opening to the diving board. I used to go up on this tower and wait hours trying to muster the nerve to dive off. Eventually I mastered it. I could do a single-somersault dive and a swan dive, but that was my entire repertoire.

There was a small lifeguard shack at the pool where the lifeguards rested. You could buy a candy bar there if you had five cents. I believe all the kids in town were down at the pool at some time during a summer day. The lifeguards were on duty from 1:00 to 5:00 p.m. That was the only time our folks would let us younger ones swim.

The water was warm in those summers, this being before the dams were built upstream on the Santiam. We all learned to swim, thanks to the thoughtfulness of our city fathers. When we were older, we swam in the Santiam, Willamette, Pudding, Luckiamute, Calapooia and numerous other rivers and lakes. I don't remember anyone drowning in those days. We all became good swimmers.

Earning Money, The Early Years

I was seven when the Great Depression hit. Actually, we never had a lot of money to begin with, so being young like that I didn't notice any difference. Money was awfully tight, so we were always looking for ways to scare up an extra nickel or two. Most everything we were interested in could be purchased for five cents. Flashlight batteries, a cup of coffee, day-old pastries, cold drinks, candy bars and ice cream cones. Movies were a dime.

I sold, or tried to sell, a lot of things. In the back of many magazines were ads for different merchandise you could sell. If you filled out the coupon in the ad and mailed it to the company, they would send you the stuff to sell. You got to keep half of the money and if you sold it all, usually 25 items, you received a prize.

I sold Unguentine salve, seed packages, magazines, pencils, pens, anything I thought people would be interested in buying. Today this might seem ridiculous, but if a company could interest enough young people nationwide, this could amount to a large sum of money.

I had my best luck selling packages of needles. They came in attractive, 30 needle packs and sold for a dime. One time I won a hand-operated movie projector, but when it came the bulb was broken. We never did find another bulb for that projector. At ten years of age, this was a major disappointment.

I had a magazine route around town. I sold the Saturday Evening Post for five cents, the Country Home Gentlemen for five cents, and Collier's Weekly for ten cents. Some Saturdays I would cover the entire town and only sell three or four magazines. My dad always told me I wore out more shoe leather than I made in profit. Being as my dad was a shoemaker, I didn't worry too much about that.

Mowing lawns was another way to make some money. I had four customers. Two of them

Me, with Bud Johannsen, 1934.

paid ten cents and the other two paid 15 cents. This included the complete care of their lawns, raking the leaves and picking up any fruit or nuts that had fallen. I used a rotary push mower, which wasn't too easy to push, but got the job done. It usually took about two hours for the average lawn.

Another way to make money was cutting and splitting wood. One of my customers was Miss Ruth Wight, my fifth grade teacher. Every week I split large hunks for the heating stove and small ones for the cooking stove. I then carried it all in and deposited it in a wood box near the stoves. For all this I was paid the princely sum of four cents a week.

Everyone burned wood then, so come summertime Leo and I would put a lot of wood in people's basements, wood sheds, even into second story offices downtown. Believe it or not, a truckload of firewood could be dumped right on Main Street in front of the stairway to second story offices. Carrying a cord of wood up a long flight of stairs took a lot of time and energy, so I doubled the price to a dollar. No one ever complained. I had a near monopoly on the second story wood business, since my dear old dad's shoe shop was in the center of town, he could see right away when the wood was dumped. The city wanted it off the street in two days, so I was always there to do the job.

The most lucrative money of the summer time was picking fruit, berries, cherries, etc. Lebanon was a center for strawberries, raspberries and prunes. The farmers grew other crops, too, but these were the main ones.

There were many of strawberry fields around, so it took almost all the kids in town to pick them.

We started picking for Bill Long. His strawberry patch was on Gore Road, a mile north of town. In the late spring of 1932, the average price per carrier of six boxes (one pound to a box) was four cents with a one-cent bonus if you stayed until the picking was done. At that time there was seven of us picking in our family, my mother, Catherine, Grace, Leo, Isabell, Mary and myself. We averaged about 100 carriers a day for all of us.

The strawberries then were planted in separate hills, 24 inches apart, not strung together in rows like they are today. There were pickers all over the patch, generally in a ragged line as the picking progressed. In the middle of the season, you could pick 12 or so carriers a day, but as the season wore on and the berries thinned out, you could get only about half that.

The highlight of the strawberry picking was the ice cream feed at the end of the season. We were not used to getting ice cream, so it was a delightful treat. The strawberry season started the latter part of May and was over by the end of the second week in June. From there we moved right into raspberries.

The raspberries were all picked by the middle of July. We then had a six-week intermission until hop picking began. That was when we worked at home to gather food for the winter. In the late 30's, pole beans were introduced in our part of the valley. Beans were picked from around August 1 until the third week in August. From there we went to hop picking, generally finishing the farm work by September 21. So it was a full summer of working and swimming for us.

The money the family earned in the fields went for school clothes and books. We never got to keep any of the picking money. The schools didn't furnish any books or supplies, so it cost quite a sum to provision all of us for school. I can still see the mountains of textbooks stacked on the floors in front on the drug store counter. I never understood why drug stores sold schoolbooks.

We did get to keep money that we earned from odd jobs. One good way to pick up some loose change was from collecting returnable bottles. There was a dance hall three miles south of Lebanon, so on Sunday afternoons I would take a gunnysack and pick up all the beer and whiskey bottles people had thrown out their car windows on their way to the dance hall. A quart beer bottle was worth a nickel and a half-gallon a dime; a pint whiskey bottle was also worth a dime. Some Sundays, I collected a dollar and a half to two dollars in bottles, enough for two or three movies, a few bottles of pop and a candy bar or two.

I also peeled bark from chittum trees in the late fall. The chittum bark was sold to a local pharmaceutical agent for use in laxatives. It brought four cents a pound wet and eight cents a pound dry, so we dried most of ours. My dad made me a chittum peeling knife. One end had a curved blade to facilitate the peeling of the bark around the small trees. The chittum trees grew wild down by the Santiam River. I never knew who owned them.

For some reason, probably economic, the local prune growers all decided to take out their prune orchards in the late 20's and early 30's. We even took out the trees on our little farm. A team of horses pulled our trees down, but sad to say they did not cut them into firewood. That chore was left for Leo and me. We took a sawhorse out to the field, threw the huge limbs on to it and sawed them into 16 inch pieces. This was done with a three-foot bow saw. This was where I got even with Leo for the hard work I had to do pulling the cultivator. Fortunately, I wasn't big enough to saw, so all I had to do was sit on the wood to keep it from moving while Leo sawed it up.

There were many trees in our two-acre orchard, so this took weeks and weeks. Evidently Dad thought we had done a fine job, because we were soon sawing up prune trees all over town. I never found out how much we made for this work, as we never saw the money.

After all this we still had to put in our own wood and chop it to fit both our kitchen and parlor stoves. I never really enjoyed all this sawing, chopping and carrying wood, but I guess it didn't hurt me either. One thing, though, the work made the playtime stand out. I treasured every bit of that.

We used to compete with other kids for jobs handing out store fliers. Merchants didn't put flyers in newspapers as they do today. If a store had a sale coming up, they would hire two or three kids to deliver them to every porch in town. For this we usually received a dollar, so competition for these jobs was keen.

Again, my father being a business man and in contact with other shopkeepers in town, I usually got my share.

Haying and Threshing

As I got a little older (12 or so), I was able to get jobs with local farmers. Hay wasn't baled in those days. After it was cut and left to dry, it was windrowed. A large angle rake would drag it into rows. Then it was stacked into a haystack about 12 feet in diameter and 5 feet high. When it was ready to take into the barn, the hay wagon, pulled by two horses, was run along side the stack and two men loaded the hay onto the wagon.

Two strong men could pitch most of a haystack onto a wagon in a single, coordinated move. With one man each side of the haystack, they would stab their pitchfork deep into the stack and with a swift lift the major part of the hay was thrown on to the wagon. A second pitch would throw up the remnants. The first pitch usually carried about 80 percent of the stack.

The driver of the wagon tied off the horses' reins and restacked the hay as needed on the wagon. The load of hay would quickly build up to 10 to 12 feet high off the field. When the load was ready, everyone climbed on the wagon and the hay was taken to someone's barn.

As there were only two seats in front of the hay wagon, we had to sit on top of the load, all of 12 feet off of the ground. The hay was held in place by gravity only, so this made for a scary ride, as least I thought so.

At the barn, a large hay hook would be loaded with hay and hauled up and into the barn. The two people who had pitched the hay on the wagon would then restack it inside the farmer's haymow (the upper part of the barn). A layer of salt was sprinkled on the hay as it built up in the barn. This was to prevent spontaneous combustion in case of heat build up on semi-dry hay.

After the hay was in, the farmer's attention was turned to the different grains, wheat, oats, barley, etc. Wheat and oats were the two main grains we worked, wheat being for the humans and oats for the animals.

The grains were handled a little differently. A reaper would tie the grain into bundles, which were left as they fell all over the field. Later, we would go in the fields and hand stack them. When they were dry enough, a threshing machine would come in and the threshing commenced.

Harvest was a major affair. Neighbors would come over with their wagons to help. The threshing machine would set up in the field wherever you wanted your straw stack left. Assorted pipes, funnels, and elbows jutted from either end of the threshing machine, enabling the machine to receive the grain bundles at one end, eject the straw and chaff, and pour out separated grain at the other end. The receiving end was a continuous belt that fed the grain bundles into the interior of the thresher.

Once the thresher was positioned, a tractor would come in to power the thresher. It used a long, long belt, nearly 200 feet long. The belt ran from a large flat pulley on the tractor to another one on the thresher. The tractor had to be kept quite a distance from the thresher to keep from setting the flying chaff on fire.

Once threshing commenced, it went on uninterrupted

until the field was cleared or it got dark. The crews usually consisted of 4 or 5 wagons, depending on the field's size and how far the field was from the threshing machine. One man kept busy adjusting everything to keep the machine going, two men were needed to sack the threshed grain and move it to the grain stack. There were always at least two ladies on hand to water and feed the men.

When all was ready, the tractor was started and the big belt came up to speed. And as it did, the threshing machine came alive, every moving part in it was going full bore; it shook, rattled and roared.

Two teams fed the machine, from wagons on either side. Men with pitchforks threw bundles from the wagons on to the conveyor belt, until a wagon was emptied. Then, the empty wagon moved on and another full wagon quickly took its place.

Grain came pouring out the other end into a transfer pipe that was split to allow two gunnysacks to be hooked to the pipe. One person was a sack sewer. When one sack filled, the sack sewer switched the transfer pipe lever to pour the grain into the other, empty sack. He would then take the full sack off of the pipe, put an empty sack back on, and sew the top of the full sack, all before the other sack was filled. You had to be quick to get one sack done before the other one filled.

There was another man waiting to move the full, sewn sack to the grain sack pile. This was usually about 30 feet away from the thresher. As each full sack weighted in around 100 pounds, this was not an easy job.

The straw from this operation spewed out a 12 inch pipe that was slanted up and out at a 45° angle. It came out of the pipe so fast it flew 30 feet or so before it hit the ground.

As the threshing machine was never moved during this operation, it wasn't long before you had an enormous pile of straw. This was used all winter for livestock bedding and all year by the kids who tunneled into it, climbed over it and slid off of it, truly one of the highlights of the harvesting season. At least it was for us young folks.

Amusement, Recreation, General Tomfoolery

As you know, young people can find hundreds of ways to amuse themselves and we were no exception. In about 1930, every kid in town seemed to get into the hoop rolling business. There were always steel hoops left lying around after the wooden wheels inside them had gone to the happy forest in the sky. We put a small crosspiece on a three-foot or so "pusher" board to roll and control the hoops. The faster you rolled them, the more things you could do with them.

Eventually you could jump them over curbs, boxes or anything else that got in your way. We rolled them all the way to school, devised ways to do combat similar to a knight's joust, ran races and even tried to see who could run them farthest up a tree trunk.

A couple of years later a tire-rolling fad became popular. As strange as this may seem, we were all rolling tires to school, to town and down to the swimming hole. The tires were mostly from of Model T

Fords, about 30 inches in diameter they were just the right size for rolling. This fad did not last long, though.

Another of our major diversions was playing marbles. In order to play marbles you need smooth ground. Cement sidewalks were limited to the Main Street, but there were smooth paths everywhere. And where these paths crossed, we played marbles.

Marbles is a simple game, but lots of fun. To get started you drew a big or little ring in the smoothest ground you could find. After each player threw an equal number of marbles into the ring, you took turns shooting a marble from outside the ring, trying to knock marbles inside the ring out. Whoever knocked the most marbles out won. When the ring was large, you had to shoot from a farther distance, so it was a bit harder to knock marbles out.

When playing with the small ring, you could shoot from wherever your "shooter" landed. The shooter was a larger marble than the regular marbles, so it would have the momentum to move the marble it might hit. We also had what was called a "boulder." It was about an inch in diameter and was used for "lagging." In order to determine who would shoot first, we drew a straight line about 20 feet away and lagged (threw) the boulder down to the line. Whoever threw his boulder nearest to the line would get to shoot first.

Marbles came in many varieties. The cheapest kind was the "doughbaby," which was essentially a piece of round clay, baked and painted. The most common marble was semitransparent and had swirls of colors all through it. These came in all colors and were quite pretty.

The ultimate marble was a round agate or "aggies" as we called them. There were not too many of these, as they were expensive, at least for us. You could play the game two ways. If you played the regular way, you got your marbles back at the end of the game. But if you played "for keeps," you kept all the marbles you knocked out of the ring. Usually it was the older boys who did that. I knew one kid, Bill Ellis, who had jars and jars full of marbles he had won.

Bill went on to be a good baseball pitcher in high school, so evidently his hand-eye coordination was much better than average. During the noon hour and at recess the school grounds were covered with marble games during the late spring and early fall.

Another popular pastime at recess and noon hour at

Me (center) with friends, 1936.

school was "camel fighting." To start things off, you would choose a partner. If you were of a good size, you found a smaller partner, or if you were smaller, you looked for someone larger than you. The smaller fellow would climb on to the larger one's back and lock his legs around his larger partner's waist. The larger fellow would hold his partner's legs as tight as he could. The object of the camel fight was to upset your opponent or to tear the upper one from his lower partner.

This was accomplished by using the legs and movements of the lower fighter combined with the arms and strength of the upper one to upset your opponents. Actually, it was very close to vertical wrestling. You couldn't hit or strike each other, but pretty much anything else was OK. The initial contact was made by rushing toward each other, with the upper partner trying to grab onto to his upper opponent with out being grabbed onto by him. If this were accomplished, then the lower partner would do his best to pull his opponent over.

Most of the time the two upper partners were interlocked so the legs of the man on the ground did the main fighting. He would push, pull, jerk sideways, or move in anyway to catch his foes off balance. If the teams were evenly matched, the battle could continue for quite awhile. The real fun started when multiple teams all tried to be the last team standing. For so simple of a game, this was a lot of fun. I don't know if the young people still play this game. I haven't seen it if they do.

Mumblypeg was another diversion. This was played by first inserting your jack knife blade into the ground. Then you attempted to flip the knife up in the air and land it on the blade. If you were successful in this, you drove a wooden matchstick or twig of approximately the same size into the ground. The loser had to extract the piece of wood with his teeth. Not easy to do when only an eighth of an inch is sticking out of the ground.

Another variation that we played was trying to knock an opponent's sharp stick out of the ground. Each player made himself a sharp stick, about 24 inches long and 2 inches in diameter. The game was played by the first player throwing his stick into the ground as hard as he could. The second player would then attempt to knock down the first stick while simultaneously sticking his stick in the ground. Whoever's stick was still in the ground after such an exchange, won the game.

Sometime in the mid-1930's the game of miniature golf became popular across the country. Lebanon was no exception and soon a miniature golf course was constructed downtown. The course was built where the Downing Building is on Main Street, just across from the IOOF Lodge. Although we never had money to play it, we could see how the individual holes were designed. We decided to construct our own course. There was a large yard between the house and the barn (no lawn in those days) and it was here we decided to put our course.

It took us most of the summer. We made it a nine-hole course and by using stovepipe elbows, pieces of pipe, assorted stones and pieces of wood. We also constructed some wooden golf clubs. So when our mother got us a couple of golf balls we were in business. The course lasted two years and provided us with many a pleasant afternoon and evening.

Move to Town and River Memories

We moved to town in the summer of 1936. I was just out of the eighth grade. My dad bought a house at 150

East Grant Street. The house had been built around 1870 or 1880, with plumbing and electricity added later. The location on East Grant was a block and a half from the center of town and two blocks from my dad's shoe shop. The inside of the house was pretty well torn up. My dad installed a heavy felt lining over the rough 1x12 walls and wallpapered over that. The new wallpaper on the walls along with the new linoleum on the floor spruced things up. The house cost $1,000. We made monthly payments of $10 a month on the loan.

Although I still had to work in the fields and odd jobs about town, I never had any more farm work to do. This gave me more free time and I spent all the time I could at the Santiam River in the summer. In the winter I would go uptown to fool around. There was always someone up there to mess around with and if there wasn't I would spend my time talking to the various shopkeepers on Main Street. As I said before, this was during the Depression and business was slow. They all came out on the sidewalk in front of their store and talked to each other and anybody else who happened to be around.

I got to know them all. As I look back on that era, I can now see we were like a big, happy family. The lack of money never seemed to concern any of us as we were all in the same boat. To anybody younger than 16, this is the way things were and we thought always would be. The townspeople were close and helped each other in those hard times. I have not seen this duplicated since and I don't believe I will again.

In the summer the boys along East Grant Street used

to spend their free time at the river. Starting with myself, there was Bud Johannsen, "Hardrock" McManama, Harold Bohle, Jimmy Fisher, Jack and George Macdonald. Gordon and Cedric Wallace already lived on the river next to the railroad bridge. In the spring and fall we all went to Cedric and Gordon's house. The river split into a large island at this point, with the smaller stream running by the Wallace house. It ran slower than the main stream so it warmed up sooner in the spring and cooled down later in the fall. So every spring and fall we would end up at the Wallace place. Besides swimming, we built dams, tree houses, forts, rafts and constructed model villages in the sandy banks of the river.

We even went out there on raining and chilly days. Mrs. Wallace had a player piano in her front room, so we played that. I can still hear the piano banging out "The Stars and Stripes Forever." Mrs. Wallace was good to us; everyday we had milk and cookies that she baked. She gave us the run of the house. I was always grateful to her for this kindness.

In the summer months we swam and played up and down the Santiam, from Waterloo to the railroad bridge east of town. There were quite a few places to swim: the dam, the Waterloo falls, and a nearby place we called "Wolfs."

Wolfs was just east of the Grant Street bridge. There was a steep path down to the river, 40 feet of slippery mud, and the beach at water's edge was small, but adequate. There was an old log boom that stretched along the river. It consisted of 15 or so slippery logs joined together with rafting spikes, a relic of a bygone era when there were no sawmills in Lebanon and they had to float logs downstream to mills near Albany. These logs had become waterlogged and slick with age. They could be difficult to stand on and more difficult to run the length of, but that is one game we played at Wolfs. We seldom made it all the way to the end, but it wasn't for the lack of trying.

We also took the white glass from under the lid of the Mason jars and used them to dive after. We threw them out into the river and dove to the river bottom after them, trying to grab them before coming up for air.

The Grant Street bridge and the railroad bridge were close together. Both bridges were 25 feet above the water. We used to climb out on the bridge railings and stand there for hours, trying to find the courage to jump or dive in. By the time I was 14, I was diving off them regularly. When I was 16, I even dove off of them in the dark.

The water was always crystal clear and teeming with waterdogs, fish, frogs and minnows. Sometimes we would make a pond by damming up a small inlet and filling it with these little creatures.

When you are young, carefree, sunburned and just plain summer lazy, time can go by so fast. Before we knew it, we were seniors, graduated and out in the world to take our turn at life.

My First Car

Around 1938, John Warden opened up a Nash

dealership a half block down the street from our home. As I walked to town, I passed the dealership. I often stopped and talked to the personnel. I got to know them all well.

One day they took a '28 Chevrolet sedan in trade. It sat on the back lot for a long time. I finally asked John what he wanted for it. He said I could have it for $15. It wasn't much, but it ran. I was only sixteen at the time, so I needed an adult to co-sign the title. I knew my dad wouldn't sign with me, so I talked my sister, Corky, into signing with me. I paid three dollars a week on it until I had it paid for. While I was waiting to take possession, I painted the car and the wooden wheel spokes black.

I parked it the next block over from our house so my dad wouldn't see it. This worked fine for about six months, until my dad found out about it.

The manner in which he cornered me about it was amusing as I look back on it. He never told me he had found out about it. All he said was, "That will be a dollar day come Monday." That was on a Saturday. I knew what he meant. My two oldest brothers, Pete and Nick, were each paying a dollar a day for room and board in our house at that time.

I caught his drift right off. He figured if I could afford my own car, I could afford to pay room and board like Pete and Nick. Meanwhile I was still a junior in high school and earning only four dollars a week working for Cap Kuhn at his local movie house. I may have been dumb, but I wasn't stupid. I immediately drove that '28 Chevy to the wrecking yard on Second Street and sold it for ten dollars. The proceeds were used to purchase a new overcoat at Reeves clothing store. Thus ended my first automobile experience. I might add that in the preceding years Pete and Nick had each totally wrecked a family car, so after that, Leo, Norm and I didn't get to drive the family car at all.

An interesting aftermath to this was my purchase of the first new car in Lebanon after the War. At that time, everybody was signing up for a new car, since none had been manufactured in the prior five years. I signed up at the Scott-Chrisman Chevrolet dealership, the Kirkpatrick Ford dealership and of course the Nash dealership of my friend, John Warden. Six months went by and nobody in Lebanon had taken delivery of a new car.

Walking by the Nash dealership one day on my home I spotted John Warden in the showroom. I went in and asked, "John, when are the new cars coming in?"

"Well Larry," he said, "nobody knows, but I will tell you what I can do. The Nash sedan has a long waiting list, but I haven't signed anyone up for the Brougham Coupe, because the factory said they weren't making any at the present time. I will put you down for one of those and we'll see what

High school senior photo, 1940.

happens."

Oddly enough, two weeks later, here came John, "Hey Larry, we just received our first new car. Believe it not it is a Brougham coupe and it's yours."

So for the princely sum of $1,608.00, I was the proud owner of Lebanon's first post-war automobile. It didn't have bumpers or a windshield wiper motor on it, but it was mine. The new bumpers didn't arrive for six months. Until then, we bolted 2x4s on the front and rear and went on our way. One of life's finer moments.

1930 TO 1940
Picking Hops in Buena Vista

Hard Times

The Great Depression was a time of anxiety and worry for my parents. After the stock market crashed in 1929, a general business malaise settled across the country. People lost jobs and banks failed. The effects were dramatic for my father, who ran a small shoe shop in Lebanon. His shop income dropped from an average of $55.00 a week in 1928 to just five or six dollars a week by 1930.

There was no bank insurance in those days, so if your bank failed, you lost all the money you had on deposit with them. Many people lost their money and their jobs at the same time. Since most families had only one income, the effects could be devastating. Fortunately, we had ten acres of good land to farm.

Our family situation still changed dramatically. There were ten of us children, ranging from two to twenty-four. My two oldest brothers were unable to find work. We had always worked in the fields, weeding row crops, picking strawberries, raspberries, prunes, cherries, walnuts and filberts. This fieldwork took up much of our summer, but was usually done by mid-August. The money we earned in the fields was used for school clothes, books and miscellaneous household expenses.

In 1930, though, the pay for picking a six-box carrier of strawberries dropped to four cents from fourteen cents the year before. Other fieldwork payments suffered similar drops. I was seven at that time, so this was over my head, but it was catastrophic to my parents.

In light of these new realities, my parents decided we would pick hops for some extra income. Hops were harvested from mid-August through mid-September. School didn't start until the third week of September, so the timing worked out nicely. Hops were a major crop in the Willamette Valley at that time, but the nearest hop field was ten miles north of Albany, near Buena Vista. Cars at that time were used only for extremely necessary trips, so we would stay in Buena Vista, camping at the hop yard, until the season was over.

Camping at the Hop Yard

In August, during one supper, my father said, "I have a surprise for all of you. Next week you're all going to the Irvine hop yard near Buena Vista to pick hops. Early hops will start next Tuesday so I will drive you up on Sunday. This will give you time to set up camp and be ready to pick Tuesday morning."

You cannot imagine the elation that swept around the supper table. We were used to hard work, so that was no concern. About the only words we heard were "set up camp." None of us children had seen a hop field. Twenty-five miles was a long way to drive in 1930, farther than most of us had traveled up to then. This would be the first honest to goodness adventure most of us would have. To say we were excited would be an understatement; we were wide-eyed. Our mother started getting things ready, assigning each of us jobs. At only seven, my main job was staying out of the way so the others' tasks could be quickly completed.

The hop yard would furnish two wall tents and a tarpaulin. We had to bring everything else. We had a 1924 Dodge touring sedan at the time. Since eight of us were going, things would be tight in the car. We removed the rear seat and stowed food on the floor of the car. We laid blankets on top of the food boxes. The Dodge had large running boards, so we used these to carry utensils, boxes of clothes, etc.

We tied a bedspring to one side of the car since my mother and sister Corky (nicknamed for the wooden leg she used in place of the one she lost to polio at twelve) needed a better bed than the ground. All these preparations only heightened my interest and I couldn't wait to get going. We finally left on Sunday, August 17, after Mass.

My father was to take us to the campground, help unload and drive home that afternoon. He was to come and get us on September 17, by which time – hopefully – we would have made a lot of money. We motored up Highway 20, past the Cottonwoods dance hall to Albany. Crossing the Willamette River at Albany, we continued several miles north on the gravel road parallel to the Willamette until we reached the Luckiamute River. Immediately after crossing the Luckiamute we spotted a hop field on the right and a grove of tall fir trees on the left.

That was our hop yard. The campground was in the fir grove, a beautiful spot. There was a large area under the trees for camping and we soon picked a good site, away from the gravel road to keep the dust down, but not too far from the well.

My mother and I went up to the Irvine house, across the road, and signed us in. We collected our tents and tarp and returned to our campsite. By this time, everything was unloaded. While my father, brother Leo, and sisters Grace and Isabell, erected the tents, I dug a pit for our cooking fire. I dug a trench so the fire itself would sit below ground level and covered most of it with the lid from a 55-gallon drum. I slanted the trench in front to facilitate feeding the fire and left a hole in the back for the smoke to escape. The fire pit was oriented to the prevailing wind so smoke would come out

Family camp at hop yard near Buena Vista, 1939. Photo courtesy of Salem Public Library Historic Photograph Collections.

downwind.

We used this fire pit continually over three weeks for cooking and heating. It worked great. Besides helping with picking, my sister Mary and I were responsible for keeping the camp in water and firewood. The well was at the Irvine house, about 300 feet away. We used our butter churn to carry the water. It held about four gallons and had a handle on each side. The top of the churn narrowed at the throat so it took a good deal of agitation to lose much water. We usually managed to arrive at the camp with at least three gallons.

The woodpile was about as far away, so in addition to having to split the wood, we had a good ways to haul it. Each day's use required four trips for water and two for wood. It was enjoyable work, though. Along the way we got to meet many other boys and girls doing the same chores, so we were soon acquainted with most of the campers.

We set our tents up opposite one another with a 12-foot space between them, over which we stretched our tarp. The campfire was under the tarp between the tents. With a good fire, it made for a snug camp even when it rained. To make a bed, we staked 2x8s on edge, then filled the space between the 2x8 and the tent wall with straw from the Irvine barn. Over this we put blankets and we were in business. This effort took all of Sunday afternoon and most of Monday, after which Mary and I went exploring, while the older girls helped our mother with kitchen work.

There were 36 picker campgrounds, all in various stages of completion. We stopped and talked to most of them. By nightfall we had made many new friends. Most of them were like us, experiencing hop picking for the first time. On Tuesday morning the camp came alive early as everyone prepared breakfast to eat and lunch to take to the field.

Growing and Picking the Hops

Hops grew differently than most crops. They grew on wire trellises, climbing up to 12 feet above the ground. The poles supporting the wire trellises were spaced about 40 feet apart, with a heavy wire stretched between them, running east and west, from pole to pole. The hop vines grew in rows on wires running north and south, hung under the pole wires. Hops' fruit resembled a small fir cone, very light and fluffy, with a pungent odor. The vines were strong and coarse. If you picked them without hand protection you would soon wear the skin off your fingers. So you either had to wear gloves, which wore out quickly, or tape your thumb and the two adjoining fingers with friction tape. Taping lasted about a half-day and gloves around four days. If you were serious about picking, you used tape.

Hop field rows were long, some of them taking three or four days to pick. When picking was started, the vines had to be lowered. This was done by dropping the row wire into "jacks," about the height of the pickers. A jack was a scissor-like support made from two 2x6s, bolted near one end. When the long end of the scissor was opened and placed on the ground, the wire holding the hop vines could be supported in the small V at the top of the jack. The weight of the vines held the wire in the jack and the jack firmly in place on the dirt. As the poles were far apart, two or more jacks were generally used to support the lowered row wire. Only enough row wire would be let down at one time, say 50 feet, to allow for two to three hours picking. When the hops were picked, a yard employee, called a dayman (because he was paid by the day) would

My brother, Norm, with our cousins, Tom and Ted DeRush, in a hop field, 1939. Note the jacks on the row behind the boys.

cut the vines off the wire and the row wire would be placed back on the hook under the pole wire.

Another dayman, called the wireman, was responsible for unhooking and dropping the row wires into the jacks. He was constantly working from one side of the yard to the other, letting vines down as the pickers needed them. He would position the jack so the wire fell into the jack's small V when it was dropped from the pole wire hook. There was a tremendous load on these wires, so the pickers stood back as the wireman unhooked them. He used a long pole with a small iron head on it to accomplish this task. On one side of the head there was a small notch to hold the large pole wire and a six-inch long pick to slide under the row wire. By leveraging the pick, he could raise the row wire out of the hook and with a twist, release it so it fell into the waiting jacks. Most of the time the wire dropped into the jacks, but if it didn't it was almost impossible to raise it high enough for picker comfort.

Any time a picker wanted a row wire lowered for picking, he or she would call out, "Wireman!" The wireman would show up, and down would come the hop-filled vines. Needless to say, all of us young fellows wanted to grow up enough to get a wireman's job.

The hops were picked in hop baskets. These baskets were round, about 30 inches deep, with a lower diameter of 16 inches flaring out halfway up to a 24 inch top. They were constructed of wood lathe and wire and were light and sturdy for their size. They held about 25 pounds of hops when full. When a picker filled two of them he would call out, "Weigh 'em up!" and the weighboss and two weighmen would come over and weigh the hops.

Hop picker near Eola, 1939. Photo courtesy of Salem Public Library Historic Photograph Collections.

The weighmen weighed the hops by emptying the

baskets into a sack and hoisting the sack on to a scale, hung from a portable tripod. The weighboss would then punch the weight into the picker's ticket and move on, with scale and tripod, to the next picker requesting, "weigh 'em up." Meanwhile, the two weighmen carried the full sack down the row to where the truck could drive under the vine-free wires.

The weighboss was also the fieldboss and was responsible for the field discipline and seeing to it that no leaves larger than a silver dollar were put in the basket with the hops. This was a constant, though amusing, struggle between the pickers and the fieldboss because the dirtier you picked, the faster you could fill a basket. You weren't supposed to "water" the hops either. Watering was dumping a canteen of water onto the hops just before you called for the "weigh 'em up".

For every pound of hops we picked, we earned one-half cent. So as I could only pick four baskets a day, I might make fifty cents. Part of this money went for gloves or tape and part of it went to the pop man who came around on hot, sweaty afternoons to offer kids soda pop for a nickel a bottle. There was lemon-lime, raspberry, strawberry, root beer, orange and mint. All ice cold and very tempting. The pop wagon at our yard was pulled by a little donkey that drank nothing but water.

There was also a water wagon that came through the field. It had a wooden barrel full of water and a wooden spout at the bottom of the barrel that protruded beyond the pickup bed. This arrangement facilitated the filling of personal water jugs, usually quart canning jars with lids that the pickers brought along. There was also a tin drinking cup attached to the barrel. Everyone drank from the same cup. Nowadays that might be considered unsanitary, but I don't recall anyone getting sick from it.

As a day wore on, some of the rows might have a heavier crop on them or maybe a few pickers would fall behind. This prevented the dayman crew from going back and forth across the yard easily and quickly for picker assistance. So to keep the hop yard harvesting reasonably aligned, the faster pickers might be pulled off of their rows temporarily to assist slower pickers. Thus the entire group of pickers would be roughly parallel to each other.

Hop Field Recreation and Pastimes

The picking would start at dawn and continue until around 5:00 p.m. When we kids had picked at least four baskets or at three o'clock, whichever came first, we would knock off and go swimming. As luck would have it, the Luckiamute River ran past the field and under a steel bridge before making a right turn north, skirting the west side of the campground as it continued its way to the Willamette River. We were used to the clear mountain water of the Santiam River, so the muddy Luckiamute wasn't the best swimming, but it was convenient.

The Luckiamute originated in the Coast Range foothills and meandered through heavily tilled valley farmland. It was murky with soil runoff and you couldn't see much through it. It was bordered on both sides by heavy undergrowth and was so shallow in most places that we were unable to swim. But there was one place, just south of the hop yard, where the underbrush had been cleared, and a large pool of deeper water made for good diving, though the water depth had to be carefully ascertained ahead of time because of the muddy water. We felt fortunate to have this one good swimming hole. Five minutes after leaving the yard we were in the water. We were allowed to stay till suppertime, so we had a lot of water recreation.

The campers rapidly became like a big family as everyone worked and lived in close proximity. We soon knew the names of the all the kids and they knew ours. We all smelled alike too. Anyone working with hops smelled like hops, a distinct and pungent odor, especially if you weren't used to it. We looked forward to the rainy days as no picking was done in the rain and we got to amuse ourselves all day. Some other boys and I took to exploring the Luckiamute, building rafts out of downed trees, hoping to float down the river. We seldom got far before we encountered some obstacle that required effort to remove. It kept us busy and happy.

The Irvine's had built an outdoor dance floor, a square platform thirty feet on each side. This was situated just outside the camp area. There were several musicians in camp, including an excellent fiddler. Every night, around a big campfire, the musicians would begin to play and anyone that even looked like they had a little rhythm got up to dance. Everyone participated in the festivities; even those too old or too tired to dance would come to listen. They would recline on the full hopsacks, one of nature's best easy chairs.

Behind the barn, across the road from the campground,

there was a huge marsh. People didn't drain every piece of land in those days. The marsh was bordered with cattails and other water plants, making it a paradise for bullfrogs, snakes, pollywogs and other assorted water creatures. The bullfrogs were huge and the snakes were three to four feet long. We captured the frogs and guided them around with a long stick until they got tired. Then we put them back in the pond and snared a snake. We would tie a string to the snakes and parade them through the campground to the consternation of the adults and the delight of the children.

There wasn't a store at the camp. The nearest one was in Buena Vista. It was the only store there. The only reason that little community existed was because it was on the western terminal of the Willamette River ferry. It was the custom for quite a few of the young ones, me included, to wheedle permission from our mothers to make a trip into Buena Vista on the off days. This was a long walk through some good farm country.

Usually about ten or twelve of us would start off after lunch. The road went due north from the yard for a quarter of a mile, then circled and climbed up over a small round butte. After rounding the butte it straightened out to the north and passed a chicken ranch. The chicken ranch had two apple trees with juicy apples just inside the front fence, which was fortunate. But unfortunately, there were two large dogs that didn't abide trespassers.

To my seven-year-old eyes, these dogs were terrifying; their barking sent chills up my spine. The older boys developed a foolproof way to get us each an apple by distracting the dogs to the opposite end of the fence while someone hurried over the fence, picked up some big apples, threw them to us on the outside and leaped back over the fence before the dogs got to him. I never did see the owners. I don't think they cared, as they didn't pick up the apples anyway.

The rest of the trip to town was uneventful. After passing two more large farms, the road climbed a mile along a hill, turned to the right past a filbert orchard, then left, and there we were.

The Buena Vista general store had a little bit of everything. We were mainly interested in candy and soda pop, of which they always had a good supply. The road continued past the store to the next town, Independence, but just past the store it forked, with the right fork leading down to the Willamette River and the Buena Vista ferry landing. The river was about 400 yards wide at this point with another ferry landing on the opposite bank. The Buena Vista ferry ran between these landings, held against the swift current by an overhead cable. The cable was anchored at each end by large towers. The ferry cable had a large block on it, with the block's pulley running back and forth over the main cable as the ferry traversed the river.

The ferry could hold six cars or two farm wagons or trucks. Foot passengers rode free and we had many a pleasurable ride on it. The walk back to camp took about an hour and a half, so we always left the ferry in time to get home for supper.

With all these activities, time passed quickly. Soon the

hop fields were picked and the feel of fall was in the air. It was time to go home and get ready for school. My father showed up one day. We all pitched in to tear the camp down and we loaded it into the Dodge. After saying goodbye to our friends, with a vow to return next year, we drove home.

Later Years

The next two years at the hop yard went well. Most of my old friends from the year before returned so we didn't waste time setting up camp. We were soon off renewing old acquaintances, catching up on happenings since we had last seen each other. Each year we were a little older, hopefully a little wiser, so our hop picking earnings increased along with our activities. Sometimes we were able to hitch a ride to Albany to see a movie and once I went in to Independence to a midget car race.

In 1933, we had a bad year. It started raining on the fourth day and never stopped. The hop vines were constantly wet and developed a mildew that attracted the hop mites. These little devils were everywhere; the vines were greasy with them. It didn't matter much, as there was no market for the infected hops. We waited around for two weeks hoping the rain would quit, but it never did. In some parts of the yard, the weight of all the water and strong winds blew vines down. Many hop poles fell over, taking rows of hops with it. That year we came home with total of $8.23.

The following year, 1934, we moved to the Krebs' hop yard. Their yard was on the opposite side of the Willamette River, about two miles east of Buena Vista.

The Krebs' yard was much bigger than the Irvine's. There were two rows of cabins on the site, with room to pitch tents nearby. The cabins had two wooden platforms for sleeping. In addition to this, there was a metal camp stove with two burners and a small oven. The stove rested on a built up platform with dirt on it. There was also a built-in table and two benches. The cabin was about the size of a contemporary pickup camper.

With this setup, we needed to pitch only one tent, which we did in the field near the cabin door. The whole arrangement was more comfortable for my mother and Corky. We soon became good friends with Wally and Bill Krebs, owners of the hop yard. Wally and Bill had a small store on the end of the first row of cabins and it wasn't long before Corky had the job of running the store. They carried everything a general store carried: groceries, tobacco, pop, gloves, tape, and even a few magazines. They also carried a good line of chocolate bars. Needless to say the store was a very popular place after the day's picking was over.

When I was 12 years old, my short smoking career began. As we were accustomed to going to the Buena Vista store every few days, we were exposed to pretty packages of tailor-made cigarettes. In those days anyone could buy cigarettes and most of the adults smoked. A bunch of us boys bought a five-cent sack of Bull Durham. We tried to roll our own cigarettes and save money like some of the men at camp were doing. But by the time we had taken a puff or two, all the tobacco fell out of the paper, so we moved on to the tailor-made cigarettes, like

Wings. These were ten cents for a pack of twenty. Like most kids, we thought we were grown up and "big time" when we smoked.

This lasted for a week, until I went to swim one day after work. While I was at the swimming hole I saw a young man about my age swim across the Luckiamute underwater. When I saw this, I remarked involuntarily, "I would do anything if I could do that." His mother was nearby and happened to overhear me.

She answered back, "Young man, if you quit smoking those cigarettes, it wouldn't be long before you could do that, too." What she said struck me. I reached into my pocket, withdrew the cigarettes, threw them in the river, and then threw the one in my mouth after them. Before that season's picking was over, I could swim underwater across the river, too.

When I was 14 years old, Bill Krebs gave me a day job. I was a wirecutter, because I went behind the pickers, cutting empty vines from the row wire with a machete. This was a dandy job: not only did I earn a dollar a day, but as I roamed across the field I could talk to all the girls.

There wasn't a place to dance at Krebs, but there was a large bonfire and lots of music at night. With an accordion, two fiddles and a guitar in action, it made for a rousing good time. People would recline on the full sacks of hops waiting to go to the dryer.

By then I had friends who were old enough to drive. Whenever they could con their folks out of the car, we would take the ferry to Independence to watch a movie. Every Friday night there was a midget car race in

Independence, which was very popular. There was no convenient bridge across the Willamette River, so if you didn't catch the ferry before ten o'clock, you had a thirty-mile detour over gravel roads with a lot of sharp, 90° turns. The cars' headlights weren't too bright in those days, so it made for fancy footwork on the brake and throttle before we finally got back to camp.

We returned to the Krebs' hop yard every year after 1934. My last year was 1940, before my 18th birthday. About 90 percent of the pickers came back every year. As I got older, I worked my way up to other day jobs, next to wireman, then to "weigh 'em up" crew, and finally in 1939 and 1940 to fieldboss, where I was in charge of all fieldwork and punching the picker tickets. There were supposed to be only about 50 pounds of hops, two baskets full, in the sacks. But most people kept punching the hops down in the basket while they were waiting for the "weigh 'em up" men. Some of the sacks weighed in at 75 pounds, which is a handful for two men, actually boys, to lift up to the hook on the scale. The hook on the scale was set high because the sacks sagged so much it was hard to keep the bottom of the sack clear of the ground.

The older we got, the more adventurous we became. After we grew tired of riding the Buena Vista ferry, we started swimming across the Willamette upstream from the ferry. It was quite a distance and the current on the east side ran at a good clip. We usually started on the western, Buena Vista, side of the river. When we were three quarters of the way across, we came to the swifter current. We tried to start far enough up river to allow for

Buena Vista ferry, 1939. Photo courtesy of Salem Public Library Historic Photograph Collections.

downward drift with this current. By the time we reached the other side, we were near the ferry landing.

Sometimes we would hike way up river, loosen an old snag, and push it into the river. Then we would float down stream hanging on to it.

When we came to the ferry we would cast off and swim to the nearest bank. I don't think the ferry operator was too fond of some of our adventures, but he never complained to us.

One year a bunch of college girls came to camp. By this time my day job required covering the entire hop field, so it wasn't long before I was acquainted with them. Being they were a few years older than I was, they seemed quite sophisticated.

About dark one evening, around the campfire, one of them turned to me and asked, "Have you ever been snipe hunting?"

"No!" I replied, "never have. In fact, I don't even know what a snipe is."

"It's a small bird, about the size of a pigeon," the girl said. "We are going snipe hunting tonight and we were wondering if you'd like to go with us?"

I picked right up on this, never having had an offer to join in any enterprise with girls, especially college-aged girls. I was flattered just to think about it. Seeing my eagerness to join in, they all got up to prepare for the hunt.

"First thing we each have to do," said another, "is get a flashlight and a gunnysack." The two necessary items were easy to come by and it wasn't long before we were equipped and ready to go.

"Now here is how you do it," one of the girls told me. "We each fan out into the field, making a big circle, go out two hundred yards or so. Drop down on one knee, hold your sack open with one hand, put the flashlight down into the sack with the other hand and turn it on."

With a reassuring smile, she said they would all fan out in a circle and do the same thing. After the bags were full of snipe, we would meet again back at the campfire.

With those words, they all departed for their assigned areas and I was left all alone in the dark. I dropped to one knee, opened my sack, popped in the flashlight and waited. And waited. And waited some more. I suppose I waited more than an hour before it came to me that these college girls were having fun at my expense.

To say that I was embarrassed is putting it mildly. I was mortified to think that a smart boy like me (my opinion) could swallow such downright tomfoolery. But they had seemed so sincere!

After arriving at this decision, how was I to get out of it. I saw only two ways: either sneak back to my bed, listen to the campfire laughter at my expense, and take my deserved derision tomorrow, or go back to the campfire and immediately swallow the bitter pill of stupidity. I chose the latter course.

I had never heard such laughter and carrying on; everybody in the camp was in on it. They were all waiting for my appearance with my empty sack and dead flashlight. Admittedly, I was a cocky kid. I deserved all I got and I got plenty. But it was episodes like this that made for good comradeship and fun.

1943
Training for War

The Shasta Daylight to Los Angeles

Three days out of Portland, the *Shasta Daylight* coasted into Los Angeles' Union Station and stopped with a final, car-rattling shudder. If a casual observer had stopped to look, they would have noticed the prevalence of young men on board. The *Shasta Daylight*, the Southern Pacific's premier run from Seattle to Los Angeles, was at war, along with every other American machine that could move men and materiel or manufacture weaponry.

This run had been gathering the pride of the Pacific Northwest, young men from Butte, Montana to Seattle and Portland. In Portland, she stopped only long enough to board another load of eager young men on their way to destinies yet unknown. The Daylight was used to this, if the young men weren't. It made this same run every three days, with a new load of volunteers and draftees for the training camps in Southern California and Arizona.

It was January 3, 1943, thirteen months since Japan blasted her way into the American consciousness at Pearl Harbor. That cowardly act shocked America and the entire nation joined as one, with a single goal of taking the battle to the enemy as quickly and as forcibly as possible. From every American city, town and farm arose a mighty roar of indignation, the likes of which this world had not seen. It culminated in a frenzied build-up of men and war machines. I was now part of this build-up, a young man of twenty, from a little town in Oregon's verdant Willamette Valley.

The *Daylight* carried men for all branches of the military. I was bound for the Army Air Corps, having dreamed of flying much of my life, nurtured by stories of Charles Lindbergh and World War I flying aces. I was able to join the Air Corps only after the military relaxed pilot prerequisites from two years of college to simply the successful completion of rigorous mental and physical tests.

I was working for Boeing in July 1942, when a friend greeted me with: "Hey, Larry, you can sign up now. You don't need two years of college any more." I dropped my tools on the spot, reported sick and hurried to the nearest Naval recruiting office. My brother, Nick, had been in the Navy from 1932 to 1939 and I wanted to be a Naval aviator. I was so excited, though, that I couldn't get my blood pressure below 140. After several hours of waiting and rechecking, the medical ensign told me, "We are not going to get you below 135. Why don't you go across the hall to the Amy. They take flight candidates up to 140." He was right, they did. They were glad to get me and I was glad to sign on with a branch that would let me fly!

It was another six months before they could accept and train me. But at last, there I was, stepping off that train, in Los Angeles, a suitcase in hand and a bewildered look on my face.

Uncertain where I should go, I flowed with the crowd out of the station. You would have to have seen it to believe it, but the street in front of the station was filled with Army six-by-six trucks. It didn't take long to find a group of them with "Santa Ana Army Air Base" stenciled on their bumper. I jumped aboard, took an end-seat on one of the benches that lined both sides and, once loaded, we were on our way.

If anyone had told me then that ten months and fourteen days later I would fly a P-38 over Los Angeles, I would have shaken my head in wonder, but that is exactly what happened.

Santa Ana, California

It wasn't hard to tell when we reached the base. There was an imposing gate, with arched sign, anchored by two concrete and brick pedestals, with large steel letters. Standing to either side were two aviation cadets in full dress uniform, with M1 rifles on their shoulders. After a preliminary inspection, a guard opened the gate and we drove in.

Some cadets were lounging around inside the gate. Seeing us drive in, they gave us the old raspberry and yelled, "Suckers! Suckers! Suckers!" as we passed.

Being at the back of the truck, I asked one of them, "How long you been in the service?"

"Three days," he replied. He was the first veteran I had come in contact with, so I was duly impressed.

After we jumped off of the truck at the Parade Grounds, they lined us up. A Captain Gates called us to attention. "Boys," he said, "you belong to me now. Forget your mothers, forget your girlfriends and your wives. For the next nine weeks you are mine. If you are lucky, in six weeks you will get a four hour pass, that is if I am satisfied with the effort you are all putting out."

Those were the last kind words I heard for two months. First they marched us to the Commissary and issued us a thin, used flight suit. Then they marched us to what they called a "barracks." If it hadn't had a small porch and a few windows, I could have mistaken it for a barn. I drew an upper bunk, near the barracks door, which was constantly opening and closing. Each barracks housed a squadron of cadets.

The staff sergeant appeared from the only private room in the barracks and said, "Gentlemen, take off your clothes and put on that flight suit. Pack up your civvies and send them home."

I took him at his word, peeled off everything but my shoes, donned the flight suit and got rid of my civilian clothes. This turned out to be the first of many mistakes I would make there, because we weren't issued uniforms or underwear for another ten days, and the weather turned cold and rainy for a week. Wearing that thin flight suit was little better than running around naked. No heat and no sympathy.

A little later they marched us to the mess hall and fed

us before they let us off for the night. I went to my bunk to rest and was amazed to look at a framing two-by-four next my bunk and see a grading stamp: "McPherson Lumber Co. Lebanon, Oregon, Grade 1." The McPherson sawmill was next to my Dad's old farm, south of Lebanon, where I spent most of my tender years. I felt strangely at home.

For the next two weeks, the days were filled with four hours of drill practice and two hours of calisthenics, plus various medical exams, immunizations, and dental visits. The dental work was something else. If you had cavities, they quickly filled them; if you had impacted wisdom teeth, they promptly pulled them. You may have been in a state of shock by the time it was over, but your teeth wouldn't need attention for three or four years, which was what they wanted.

I lucked out on the dental work, having had it done in 1941, while I was working for Lockheed in Burbank. That job at Lockheed had been my first steady job, fifty-three cents an hour, with time and a half on Saturday and double time on Sunday. And at that time everyone worked seven days a week. With my first week's wages I bought a '33 Chevrolet Cabriolet convertible, a nice car.

For those next two weeks, as we endured the shots, the dental work, and the near freezing to death, we were a sad looking squadron.

One morning during that first week, the duty sergeant stuck his head into our barracks door and hollered, "Any experienced truck drivers in here?"

Not wanting to pass up an opportunity for a brief vacation from drill and calisthenics, I quickly answered in the affirmative. After he had rounded up four more eager beavers, he gave us our driving instructions: "You guys drive over to the mess hall, tell the mess sergeant I sent you over for deep sink detail."

And that sink was deep indeed! Deep, long and wide! It was deep enough to hold the enormous pots the mess cooks used to feed, well, to feed an army. We started at 8:00 that morning with ten bars of soap, five double-ended scrapers, about fifty scouring pads, and an unlimited supply of hot water. After what seemed an eternity, the last pot was finally scoured to the mess sergeant's satisfaction. "Hey, you guys are fast," he told us, "sometimes they don't get done till midnight!"

I glanced at the clock. It was 11:20 p.m. If I hadn't been so worn down, I would have cried. That being only my fourth day in the squadron, I was amazed how much I had already learned: not to volunteer and the fine art of deep sink diving.

Little more than a week later I faced yet another learning opportunity, one that caused me to look back at sink diving with nostalgia: guard duty. Every soldier pulls guard duty, but putting ten-day, tenderfoot cadets on base perimeter with loaded M1 Garands would have been risky if there actually had been anything to guard against.

The only instructions they gave us were to put the rifles over our right shoulders and march. When we asked, "Where?" we were told, "from here to there and back, and then from here to there and back again, and again, for four hours."

After four hours, we would be given a four-hour break,

to rest. Then it was back to "here to there" for four more hours, and so on, until our twenty-four duty elapsed. They weren't specific about where "here" or "there" were, only that we should march until you saw the next guard walking toward us, then turn around and march back. It didn't seem difficult, except that it was dark and how was I to see the next guard in the dark?

We were assigned arbitrary post numbers. I was the guard at post 9. Every so often I heard someone yell, "Corporal of the guard, post number 2 [or 3 or 4]!" After post 8 called out, I figured it was my turn, so I hollered "Corporal of the guard, post number 9!" I never saw a corporal, but I did see a general.

A few hours into my uneventful shift, a jeep approached my post. I jumped into the middle of the road in front of the jeep, put my rifle at the ready and shouted: "Who goes there?" The jeep stopped. I stood there in its high beams, while the soldier driving the jeep stepped out and stood beside the Jeep, in the dark. But even in the dark, I could make out the star on his collar and loops on his shoulders.

"Soldier," he said, "let's see you go through the entire Manual of Arms."

I had never seen the manual, let alone memorized it, so I snapped to attention with the rifle at my side. This failed to impress him.

"Soldier, how long you been in this man's army?"

"Eleven days, sir," was my feeble response.

"Well, let me show you how this is done. First, when a vehicle approaches, stand to the side of the vehicle's path, in the dark. Stop them, let them get out and stand *them* in front of the headlights. This way they will not know how many of you are out there. And, if they look a trifle shady or are wearing a Jap or a German uniform, you can call for help. Now, doesn't that seem logical?"

Of course he was right, but this was all happening pretty fast for me.

"Here," he said, "Give me your rifle, you get in the jeep and I'll show you the proper way to stop a vehicle." And he did. That was the first and last time I received instructions from a general.

In time, I did learn the correct Manual of Arms and how to march properly. It amazed me how many men could move in an orderly manner if they knew how to march. And, with four hours of daily drill instruction, it wasn't long before we all knew. But after two weeks of drilling and indoctrination, we were ready for something more aviation related.

The Santa Ana Preflight School was enormous: 8,000 cadets in a nine-week course. Classes were staggered so that every four weeks 4,000 cadets graduated and left for Primary Flight School and 4,000 new cadets arrived to begin their training. Even at this enormous size, there were no disciplinary problems. No leeway on behavior was allowed and none was taken because everyone there wanted to fly.

We started with a battery of aptitude tests to see which aviation role we were qualified for: pilots, bombardiers or navigators. Of course, we all believed we were going to be pilots. I was lucky, though, and scored high enough to be given my choice of role.

After the testing was completed everybody was assigned to pilot, navigation or bombardier training and things settled down. A routine morning went something like this: reveille at 5:00 a.m., breakfast at 6:00, personal and barracks inspection at 7:00, drill and Manual of Arms from 8:00 to 10:00, and calisthenics at 10:00. We got a break at 11:00, which generally meant we were in our bunks for an hour. Lunch was at noon. At 1:00 p.m., we went to preflight classes. By the afternoon I was a little tired and sleepy, but not too sleepy because the preflight classes had to be passed with no less than a ninety percent grade. The thought of washing out of preflight for poor grades kept even the worst sluggard on his toes.

Classes were conducted from 1:00 to 5:00 p.m. and covered four topics. First, we took aviation physics, covering aerodynamics, theory of flight, atmospheric conditions and other facts and fallacies that would get us off the ground.

Santa Ana Army Air Base, November 1942.

After an hour of physics, we took up navigation. Cadets slated for the pilot schools were taught navigation by dead reckoning and pilotage. Cadets headed for navigator school studied these techniques and celestial navigation. Dead reckoning estimated your position by using elapsed flight time, airspeed, and course heading, after adjusting for the wind, since wind speed and direction affected one's actual speed and track over the ground. Pilotage was navigating through visual identification of landmarks. We studied maps and the different mapping projections, such as the Mercator, the conical, polyconical and others.

The next subject was weather. We learned the differences between various fronts, between the gentle cirrus clouds and a dangerous cumulonimbus, between an isobar and any other bar, wet, wild or otherwise. Weather was critical to flight safety, so a good deal of class time was spent on it. We all learned how to look at the clouds, check the wind direction and temperature and come up with a reasonable forecast for the next four to six hours. It was the start of an awareness of the sky that was to increase steadily during my Air Corps career.

The last subject of the day was aircraft engines, the theory, maintenance and adjustment of aircraft power. The ability to control throttle, propeller rpm, fuel/air mixture, and engine temperature were vital. The aircraft's range, maneuverability and safety depended on these controls.

The engines class ended at 5:00 p.m. and dinner was served at 6:00. Dinner was often followed by movies such as *Why We Fight,* a Frank Capra documentary series about the causes and perpetrators of the Second World War. All in all, weekdays were full days, and this continued for nine weeks, after which, if we passed, we were deployed to our respective flight schools.

Some weeks into training we were given four-hour weekend passes. Provided, that is, that we hadn't lost that privilege due to inspection "gigs." We had personal and barracks inspections every morning. The Army insisted that everything to be done to specification, even down to the last pair of socks in your footlocker. The bed had to be made tightly enough to bounce a quarter that was flipped on to it. We called our inspector "Gigger Gates" and he lived up to the nickname in spectacular fashion. He would come into our barracks wearing clean, white gloves and run his fingers over window and door moldings, any crack or crevasse he could find. If a white finger came back dirty, he gave you a gig. Every gig meant one hour of marching back and forth in front of the guardhouse, with full gear and rifle. If a squadron accumulated 10 or more gigs within one week, then that squadron lost their weekend's passes. Luckily we didn't receive many gigs.

The day finally came for our first pass. You can't do much in four hours, but we tried, oh, how we tried. As soon as we were stepped off the base bus, we headed for one of the local bars. The bar business must have been good around that base, because there were a lot of bars nearby. No four-hour pass was going to be wasted on a long bus ride and these jokers knew it. The Santa Ana Army Air Base was located on the outskirts of Santa Ana, south of Anaheim and the future Disneyland area.

Like all other service men we were looking for wine, women and song, though not necessarily in that order. After a fruitless search through some of the local bars, we soon learned that we would have to settle for wine and song.

One time about twenty or thirty of us ended up in one bar. As we were in the majority, we took the place over. We kept the two bartenders busy just waiting on us. A popular song at that time was "I'm Going to Buy a Paper Doll to Call My Own" by the Ink Spots. We filled that bar's nickelodeon enough to play that song fifty or hundred times. I don't know how long it lasted, but it was still playing three hours later when we left.

We also spent weekend pass hours south of the base on Balboa beach. There was a penny arcade there that was out of this world. For a penny you could watch a Parisian girl shimmy or a miniature band play "The Stars and Stripes Forever." That arcade had the most fascinating antique, coin-fed machines you could imagine.

Later in training, we were eligible for overnight passes on Saturday night. We had to be back Sunday by noon for the Pass in Review parade. These were parades of marching cadets similar to those you may have seen West Point or Annapolis cadets marching in. All the Santa Ana cadets marched in Pass and Review every Sunday. I enjoyed marching, and I especially enjoyed it with when accompanied with marching music. A couple of times we marched in review before a grandstand filled with dignitaries while a band played the Army Air Corps song.

It was a beautiful sight to see eight thousand men move as a unit on such occasions. People came from miles around to watch these Pass in Review parades.

Overnight passes normally released us Saturday afternoon, at 4:00 p.m. On Saturday mornings, though, track meets were held with five other squadrons and the winning squadron was allowed to start their weekend pass earlier, at 1:00. We happened to have a former college track star, Jim Walters, in our squadron. Jim ran the 100, 220, 440 and 880 for us. He won every race, every time he ran, though he would always end up writhing on the ground with charlie-horses by the last race. Through our entire time at Santa Ana, thanks to Jim Walters, our squadron won every meet and usually won by a large margin, so we left base at 1:00 on Saturday afternoon, instead of 4:00.

It was the custom for cadets to go into Los Angeles and stay at the Biltmore Hotel and we of course continued that tradition with all the gusto we could muster.

Transportation was a problem, though, because it was forty miles to Los Angeles. As cadets, we were paid only $75.00 per month and couldn't afford too many taxi rides into Los Angeles. We solved this problem by getting six or eight of us together, heading to a nearby used car lot and buying a junker we figured would get us through the night. All we wanted to know was if it would start and if the lights worked. We could pick up a '33 or '34 Plymouth or Chevy for around $75.00. After we finished with it, we left it along the road, outside the base. I used this same scheme at later flying schools since the airfields always seemed to be located ten or more miles from town. I often wondered what happened to those old cars, if the used car lots got them back and resold them. We never had papers on any of the cars in those days.

During one of these weekends, in February 1943, I ran into an old friend from Lebanon, Harold Post. Harold had just graduated from P-38 fighter training and was about to leave for Europe. I wanted to fly a P-38 myself so I was very interested in everything Harold had to say.

A few months later in May, I read in the *Lebanon Express* that Harold Post was killed in action over southern Italy. I am sure that I was the last Lebanon person to see him alive. It brought the danger of war into sharp focus for me and I resolved to devote every opportunity to advancing my knowledge and flying skills as thoroughly as possible.

King City, California

By the end of Preflight Training, everyone was getting anxious to fly – nine weeks in the Army Air Corps and we had yet to see an airplane! On March 10, 1943, I was one of 180 happy cadets boarding chartered buses for King City, California.

The King City Primary Flight School was situated in the Salinas Valley, about 30 miles south of Salinas, California. The airfield was on a mesa, with terrain at either end of the field dropping off a few hundred feet. The King City flight school was an Army contract school, run entirely by civilians. The only Army personnel on site were the check pilots. The check pilots gave cadets a "check ride" every two weeks to assess their learning progress. If you didn't pass a check ride, you were through, "washed-out" was our word for it. You could apply for gunnery school and still fly on bombers, but who wanted to do that when you could zoom around the skies in your own fighter and wear gold bars on your lapel.

Each instructor was assigned six students. They were his students for the next nine weeks, the entire primary training schedule. My instructor was Larry Hunt, a former World War I pilot who had continued flying ever since. He was a crackerjack instructor and I was glad to have him. My first ride was a get acquainted ride. It was only the second airplane ride I had ever taken.

My one previous flight had been a turn over Albany when I was twelve. Tex Rankin and his Flying Circus came to Albany every summer. In the 1930s, this was powerful stuff to a youngster with dreams of flying and I never missed a show. It was at one of these shows that Evelyn Burleson, a famous lady pilot of the time, was giving rides in a Waco biplane for one dollar. I told her that I only had ninety-nine cents, but was sure hankering for a ride. "Close enough," she said, and we were airborne in no time. Even though we landed ten minutes later, my head was in the clouds for weeks.

We trained in Ryan PT-22s, the prettiest vintage airplane you ever saw. It was a low-winged monoplane, with wire-braced wings to withstand any flight maneuver. It had a six-cylinder radial engine, with the cylinders extending beyond the engine cowl, giving it a racy, powerful look. The wings and tail were fabric covered and the fuselage was aluminum, with two open cockpits. The

The Ryan PT-22. Photo courtesy of www.WarbirdAlley.com.

PT-22 had a saucy, can-do appearance.

The minimum dual instruction time before you were allowed to solo was eight hours. Eleven days after starting, with eight hours and four minutes of flight time, I was ready for my first solo or at least Larry Hunt said I was.

I had been having a high time learning and practicing stalls and then spins. And, when I finally learned to recover from a spin, my instructor insisted that I be able to recover from a spin after a precise number of revolutions, on a specific heading. For example, if I didn't complete exactly two and a half revolutions and come out of the spin on a westerly heading, I was made to feel like some kind of misfit, a candidate for infantry latrine detail and generally a waste of time and gasoline to the Army Air Corps. We also learned to turn the airplane, in both shallow and steep turns at specific angles of bank. All of this wasn't that hard, it was just coming at you at a rapid rate. After eight or nine dual training sessions we moved on to flying landing patterns and to landing the aircraft.

To insure order and safety among multiple landing planes, pilots fly in a landing pattern on an imaginary rectangle above an airfield. One leg of this rectangle would be aligned directly over the runway itself and the three other legs would run about 400 yards off both ends and one side of the airfield. The normal landing protocol called for pilots to enter this pattern on the leg running parallel to the runway leg, fly down that leg (called the "downwind" leg) parallel to the runway, turn 90° left and perpendicular to the runway and then 90° left again to line up on the runway for final approach and descent to land. If all pilots observe this landing protocol and sequence their aircraft in this pattern, many planes can land safely in a short time.

Our landing pattern was, of course, full of neophyte pilots, so I kept a sharp lookout at all times. After a few hours of landing practice my instructor lifted up the speaking tube to talk to me. The speaking tube was a piece of rubber hose with a funnel on one end so he could talk to me; that's right, it was a speaking only tube, I couldn't answer. He told me: "Go over to take-off area, I am getting out." So I did and out he climbed. He patted me on the shoulder as he shouted over the engine, "I can't stand it any longer, you take her up and make three landings. I'll see you back in the ready room."

I was shaking almost as much as the airplane as I revved the engine for the take-off.

Apply power quickly. Listen to the engine. If it takes power smoothly, lay it on full. A little forward pressure on the stick to lift the tail! A little right rudder to counteract engine torque, but not too much or you may ground-loop[1] her! Then neutralize the stick as she picks up speed, so she flies herself off at around seventy miles per hour.

And fly it did! Now, all I had to do was fly the landing pattern around the field and land. Nothing to it, right?

Enter the downwind leg. Retard the throttle. Turn on carburetor heat so the carburetor doesn't ice up with the reduced throttle. Trim the elevator back to remove the back pressure from the stick. Turn left. Turn left again on to final approach. Line up with the runway. Retard the throttle a little more, judging altitude and air speed to reach the runway. As she glides over the end of the runway, pull the throttle all the way back. Hold back pressure on the stick until the final stall, which should be only inches off the ground.

Sure enough, I looked all around and I was actually rolling along the runway. What a thrill! What a relief!

I looked over at Larry and he gave me the thumbs up and waved me on again. My second landing was a pretty good one and he waved me on for my third try. But the wind direction changed and I didn't realize it. Normally, you land into the wind, but on my last try I landed downwind, with the wind. As a result, I could not get the plane to stall, it just kept flying along the runway, barely off the ground. I didn't touchdown until I was over

---

[1] A ground loop is an unintentional reversal of direction in an airplane moving on the ground. It occurs when the tail of the airplane loses directional stability, allowing the plane to abruptly change direction. It frequently causes damage to the aircraft.

halfway down the field and going too fast at that. I tried the brakes, but cautiously because if braked too severely the PT-22 could pitch forward and the propeller would chew up the ground. I was running out of runway; the fence at the end of the field was approaching very, very fast. I wasn't sure what to do. I didn't want to nose it in or ground-loop it, so I tried strong right rudder, left aileron and right brake. Somehow it worked: the plane snapped to the right and stopped.

My instructor came over laughing. "That is the fastest right turn I've ever seen!" he said. I was discouraged by the episode, but Larry coached me on my mistakes. As I left the flight line, I overheard him taking with another instructor and they were both amused by the incident.

Before I knew it, it was primary training graduation day for our class 43J. The 43 for the year (1943) and J for the month (October) we were to receive our wings. At the graduation there was a banquet where the instructors got together and roasted their fledging flyers. During the ceremony, they awarded me the trophy for being the most improved pilot. I received a $25.00 War Bond and a silver identification bracelet with my name on it. I wondered if my third solo landing had anything to do with it.

I had accumulated 65 hours in the PT-22 by graduation. About half of those hours were dual instruction and half solo hours. We were now proficient in landings, take-offs, all manner of turns, stalls, spins, and many acrobatic maneuvers (such as snap rolls, slow rolls, loops, Immelmann turns, chandelles, Cuban eights, and hammerhead stalls).

Merced, California

From King City we went to Merced, California for Basic Flight School. At Merced we flew the Vultee BT-13 Basic Trainer. The BT-13 was considerably larger and, with a 450 horsepower radial engine, more powerful than the PT-22.

After four or five hours of instruction, I soloed in it and I was on my way. Besides constant practice in the maneuvers I had learned in primary training, we had a lot more to learn, such as flying in formation (which became a source of great enjoyment for me), night flight and instrument flight.

Instrument flight training was tedious, but we learned to fly with our heads under the instrument hood. This was

BT-13s at an Army Air Corps flight school, 1943. Photo courtesy of Paul H. Krumei, www.warbird-central.com.

a black curtain that draped over the student's cockpit, creating a condition of complete blindness of the outside world; we could see nothing except our cockpit instrument panel. Our aircraft were equipped with a gyro-horizon instrument, which provided an artificial horizon for the pilot to orient the aircraft. A spinning gyroscope inside the instrument enabled it to hold the artificial horizon parallel to the actual horizon, even as the airplane maneuvered through the air, constantly changing its attitude. An artificial horizon and an airspeed indicator were all you needed to keep the plane flying on an even keel. Add a compass for your heading, the clock for your timing and you were equipped for blind flying in almost any condition.

The BT-13 was a much heavier airplane than the PT-22. For safety, we had practiced flight maneuvers in the PT-22 above 3,000 feet and above, but for the BT-13 our minimum safe acrobatic altitude was 6,500 feet.

It didn't take much to spin a BT-13. All you had to do was bring the nose up in a power-on stall, and as you stalled pull the power back, kick in the left rudder (or right, if you wanted to spin right) and hold the stick full back. The longer you held these control positions, the faster you spun. And of course the faster you spun, the longer it took to recover. To recover, you neutralized the stick, kicked hard on the opposite rudder, and waited . . . and waited for the revolutions to slow and stop.

The instant you stopped spinning and the earth below stopped flashing across your windscreen, you neutralized the rudder and the plane would be in a straight, steep dive, which was easy to return to a level flight attitude, assuming you had sufficient altitude left to do it in. Otherwise you would, as they used to say in the flying business, "auger in." There is still one more thing to watch for: if the rudder was not promptly neutralized as rotations stopped, the plane could start a spin in the opposite direction.

The first time I practiced a spin in the BT-13, I wound it fairly tight, then applied the opposite rudder to stop the spin and waited to return the rudder to neutral. Since I was a little nervous that first time, I over-controlled the rudder on the recovery and the plane yawed to the opposite side and started vibrating. It shook so violently the hand mike come off its hook and proceeded to beat me about the head and the canopy slid back. About then, I wished I had joined the infantry. Later, in discussing this hair-raising experience with my instructor, I learned why the BT-13 was nicknamed the "Vultee Vibrator."

We spent half of the day in ground school and half flying. When we had acquired a certain proficiency in flight maneuvers in the BT-13, we were introduced into night flying and formation flying. In formation flying, instead of concentrating on the horizon or your instruments, you had to concentrate on your leader's wing and use the throttle and flight controls as necessary to stay in position relative to your leader's wing. It took practice, but once you had it, you had it, like learning to ride a bicycle. The only other flying experience that came even close to the pure enjoyment of formation flying was landing. As long as I was in the Air Corps, I never tired of either.

Night flying was different. There were around 40 planes in our school, so we took turns at night flying practice. We all took-off at dusk and flew to one of the nearby auxiliary fields. These were nothing but large grass fields; it looked to me as if the Army rented a wheat field. When flying in daylight there were always eight or so planes landing simultaneously, each plane flying a slightly larger pattern than the plane inside him. At night, the landing protocol was changed to allow one airplane to land at a time. The rest would stack up at progressively higher altitudes, waiting their turn.

We kept landing in the field in this fashion until the dusk faded into night and it got so dark that all you could see was the one spotlight on a pickup truck parked near the landing end of the field. The feeble light illuminated only enough of the field so you could see where to touchdown. There was also a light at the opposite end of the field so you could line up on it for the take-off roll. It seemed to me to be a ticket to disaster, but it worked well enough. We practiced at that field for several nights without an accident. There may have been some close calls and terrifying moments, but no physical contact between any of the BT-13's.

The biggest thrill was when the word came over the radio to return to base. Everyone seemed to think that he had first priority for departure. Those 40 planes looked like a hive of hornets prodded with a stick. To this day I still wonder how these practices came off accident free.

Toward the end of basic training we were informed that on that next morning we were to fly to Deming, New

Mexico on a cross-country flight. They gave us a map, paper, pencil, and a pair of dividers to plan the trip with. Besides being good training for us, it was a pleasant break from our regular grind. It was also the first time I had flown such a long distance and over such scenic terrain. The weather and visibility were excellent. It was the first of many Air Corps "highs" that I was to know. The trip was an experience in the freedom of flight.

Not every cadet made it to Deming, though. One cadet called back to Merced from Redding, California. He said, "I thought everything was going OK until Mt Shasta loomed up in front of me!" We figured they might wash him out over this, but they didn't.

The washout rate had been fairly high in primary training, around 15 percent, but it tapered off more and more as we progressed through flight schools. I didn't know if this was because the government didn't want to waste the training they had invested or if they were just hard up for pilots. Anyway, we weren't worried about proficiency check rides anymore.

They did try to trip us up psychologically, though. One incident that stood out was a time when a major came in to our ground school class and told us that a Colonel Jenks was coming through on a Base Inspection. Then suddenly there was a knock on the classroom door and the major shouted, "Attention!"

We jumped up ramrod stiff as the colonel walked in. He was in a foul mood. He barked: "Why didn't somebody call these men to attention when I came into the room?"

Things went downhill from there. He gave us a dressing down the likes of which you would not want to hear. He walked around the classroom, silently eyeing us up and down, finally stopping and standing near the door. His mouth screwed up in a sarcastic grimace.

"Never!" he shouted, "NEVER, have I seen such a sorry looking bunch. You men are a disgrace to all that the US Army Air Corps stands for. By God, I would rather have a bunch of grade school girls than this pansy looking outfit. I am surprised they don't sew lace around your underwear . . ." This tirade went on and on (but I will not contribute to the delinquency of my readers by repeating his insults).

Finally, one cadet got fed up with the tongue-lashing, ran up to the colonel and shook his fist in his face. He told the colonel: "You dirty, rotten son-of-a-b____! I am not going to take any more of this, not from you or anybody else in this man's Army."

Evidently the colonel got what he looking for because he turned on his heel and left as abruptly as he entered. I think the Army was testing to see if anybody might crack under the strain. The cadet that barked back at the colonel left basic flight training and we never saw him again.

There was one time I thought that I might get booted as well. As I have mentioned, to insure order and flight safety we landed using the prescribed landing pattern protocol. However, as cadets, we figured the hottest thing we could do was fly a small, tight pattern. And if other cadets happened to be sequenced ahead of us in the pattern, we could show them what real hot-dogs we were by flying a still smaller and tighter pattern, cutting them off and landing ahead of them. Besides being a safety risk, this stunt could be chancy for one's ego, because if the pilot you were cutting off saw you, he would tighten his pattern and try to beat you to the ground and force you to go around again to land. Attempting this stunt and failing, that is being cut off by the pilot you were attempting to cut off, was about the most humiliating thing that could happen to a cadet. Needless to say, every cadet tried to pull this against another cadet at one time or another and I was no exception.

It was, however, my bad luck to attempt this with the base commander! I had no idea the commander was in the aircraft ahead of me. Like a hot-dog cadet, he was flying a tight pattern, but I calculated that there was a sliver of room for me to turn inside and cut him off, so I went for it. But he saw me and squeezed me tighter. I was determined not to go around, so I hung right with him and when we finally landed we were side-by-side, only 10 feet apart. But he was on the runway, while I had one wheel on the runway and one wheel on the grass.

He immediately threw open his canopy, jerked his hand up and motioned me over to the side of the runway. He stopped with me and there, in front of God and all the other cadets that I had hoped to impress, he informed me who he was and what he was going to do with me.

As I listened, I thought this was the end of my flying career! But I only got that good chewing-out and a couple laps around the field in full flight gear and parachute, on a hot and sunny July day.

I was written up for this incident in my class book and I was not allowed to participate in our graduation day flight formation, but I graduated.

Chandler, Arizona

On September 1, we left Merced for Advanced Training School at Williams Army Air Base, in Chandler, Arizona. I had 145 hours of flight time and was eager to receive those Silver Wings. Advanced flight training was a basic twin-engine flying school. When we had proven ourselves by mastering the twin-engine AT-9, we would then attend a brief Gunnery School in Ajo, Arizona. After Gunnery School, it would finally be P-38 time.

We were beginning to get a peek at the light at the end of our tunnel, but first we had to master the AT-9. This, as it turned out, was not easy for me. But I wasn't alone here; we all experienced a little trouble with the AT-9. The boys from the earlier class told us that the AT-9 took-off at 120, flew at 120 and landed at 120. There was more than a little truth in this. It

AT-9s from Williams Air Base, 1943. Photo courtesy of www.p-38.com.

had a fairly high wing loading (aviation lingo for a heavy plane relative to its wing area). High wing loading translated into weak climb and turn performance. The AT-9 took-off and landed at about 90 mph, faster than the PT-

22 or the BT-13 that I was used to, and with the high wing loading, it wasn't difficult to unintentionally stall in a steep turn, a steep climb or other violent maneuvers. But for landing, it was at least easy to bleed off airspeed. But it was an airplane, right? And we knew a little about flying airplanes.

I had the most trouble landing the AT-9. Its throttle control was in the center of the cockpit, to the pilot's right. Army Air Corps pilots were taught never to take the hand away from the throttle (good advice for any pilot). This meant that the AT-9 pilot used his left hand for the flight controls, the opposite of the throttle/flight control orientation we had learned on the PT-22 and BT-13. So, basically, I had never flown with my left hand. And, since I was extremely right-handed, it was not easy for me to get used to the AT-9.

One time during night landings I flared the controls back and stalled it while still 6 or 8 feet above the ground! It made a dreadful crunch as it I hit the runway, but the landing gear held. Even before my landing roll stopped, I heard a loud voice over the radio, "Schmidt! Take that plane straight to the mechanics and have it checked out. You're through for the night."

For whatever its flying challenges, the AT-9 was a fine looking airplane, all metal construction, with two radial engines and with engine nacelles nicely faired into the wings. We flew several cross-country flights around the Arizona desert, taking turns as pilot and copilot, without an instructor.

After about 50 hours in the twin-engine AT-9, we

moved to the AT-6 to practice aerial gunnery. The AT-6 was another single-engine trainer, with a nine-cylinder, 600 horsepower radial engine. I was back in my element with the AT-6 because its throttle/flight control orientation was what I was used to and my right hand could return to the stick. What a treat it was to fly. With all the horsepower you could want, it handled every maneuver I knew and some I didn't know and it performed them with consummate ease.

We moved briefly southeast about 100 miles to Ajo, Arizona, near the Organ Pipe Cactus National Monument, for Gunnery School. There was little around Ajo except open space and saguaro cacti, but open space was good for when the 30-caliber bullets were flying.

Our AT-6s had a single 30-caliber machine gun mounted to the right of the cockpit window. The gunnery

AT-6 over Phoenix, 1943. Photo courtesy of William T. Larkins.

target was a white, rectangular banner, towed 200 feet behind another AT-6. The honor of piloting the target tow plane went to the gunnery school cadet who screwed up worst the day before.

I learned quickly that if you wanted to hit the target, you had to be almost on top of it. We began target runs with a high wingover maneuver and dove on the target from the right, above the tow plane so the tow plane would always be in sight as you made your firing pass.

I thought I was doing pretty well coming nearer and nearer the target on each pass and getting more hits as a result. Unfortunately, I got too close on one pass, shooting and severing the tow cable only about 20 feet behind the tow plane. In addition to getting the usual lecture, I received the honor of piloting the tow plane the next day.

This was not much to my liking. If you've ever walked behind a shooting gallery or a gunnery range, you get the idea. From that day forward I kept my distance from the tow plane and my eyes on the target.

After a week of hosing 30-caliber bullets across the Sonoran Desert, we went back to Williams to finally do what we all had joined for: fly the P-38.

The P-38s we trained in were models the British had ordered, but didn't accept because their engines lacked superchargers and weren't powerful enough above 18,000 feet.

They were still awe-inspiring airplanes below 18,000 feet! They were about twice as heavy as anything we'd flown, and with four times the horsepower. At that time, they were powered by two 1,150 horsepower Allison

[90]

engines. Engine temperature was controlled manually, so you had to monitor the coolant temperature gauge, opening or closing the coolant vents as needed. We were told that this was one of the highest priorities for P-38 pilots, because overheated engines didn't last long and neither would we if the engines ever seized up.

The first time a crew chief was instructing me in engine procedures, he sat in the cockpit while I stood on the wing between the cockpit nacelle and the engine boom. When the crew chief cranked the engine up, it backfired. Smoke and flame started to blow by me and would have blown by me, except that I bolted off the wing, believing the engine was blowing up. The crew chief got a good a laugh out of it. He told me that happened with student pilots all the time and the crews were always wondering which student would be next.

We spent one whole day familiarizing ourselves with the aircraft, the instruments, switches, circuit breakers, handles, cranks and levers. There were 104 gauges and controls overall. If you were in a hurry, it was a challenge to keep track of it all. When the instructor thought we had acquired sufficient knowledge of the cockpit procedures, he gave us a piggyback ride in the plane.

To enable two people to fly together in the single seat P-38, the radio behind the pilot's head was removed. This left a small shelf the student could squeeze onto. From this position, with his body cramped and bent forward, the student's head occupied the space the pilot's head would normally have occupied. The pilot, in turn, had to lean forward, pushing his head forward into the space closer to the canopy windscreen. The resulting position was awkward to fly from and the students couldn't see much of what was going on in the cockpit.

Still, it was still better than no experience prior to attempting to solo one of these monsters. The sound and fury of those massive Allisons and the forces pulling that airframe were intimidating if you weren't accustomed to it.

The big moment arrived the next day, when we were told we would then solo a P-38. There were only about thirty P-38s at Williams Field, so we had to fly in turn. My turn didn't come until late that afternoon, when it was already 103°. The plane was hot and getting hotter when I strapped in. The instructor told me to pay close attention to the coolant temperature as they were having trouble with the engines overheating. If either engine temperature exceeded the safety threshold before it was my turn to take-off, I was instructed to taxi back and shut it down until the engines cooled down.

This happened to me twice! When I strapped in that third time, I was as hot as the coolant in those cooling condensers. I decided this time that I wasn't coming back if the coolant got too hot. Sure enough as I taxied out, in the flight line, behind the other pilots preparing to solo, both engines' coolant temperatures started to overheat. I had the coolant vents wide open, but the temperature warning lights came on. I kept my place in line anyway. Although that was 55 years ago, I still remember it clearly to this day.

When it was my turn, I lined up and pushed both

throttles forward to gather takeoff speed, which was 100 mph. I kept one eye glued on the coolant temperature gauge and the other eye on the airspeed indicator. On a plane this heavy, you do not sense the lightness that you do in lighter aircraft as the wings start to lift you off the ground. When I saw the airspeed reach 100 mph, I eased back on the control column and began to fly. But I had kept my attention too focused on the instruments, because when I looked out I had drifted to the right, into another student's airspace. Luckily no one was taking off with me, so I corrected course and kept climbing.

The take-offs are critical with twin-engine aircraft and the P-38 was no exception. If one of the engines quit on take-off all you could do is pull the throttles back and belly it in. If you tried to climb out on one engine, at less than 150 mph, the aircraft would flip over and nose into the ground. This crash was always fatal, but nothing to worry about, if you were prepared for that possibility. I never lost an engine on take-off and I was grateful for that.

Once in the air, with the landing gear and flaps up, the 38 came alive. There is no way I can describe the feeling of power. We were told to make a two-hour flight to get the feel of the plane and that was two hours of sheer excitement.

As I approached the field to land, entering the landing pattern, I made a high climbing turn to the right to bleed off air speed and lowered the landing gear and the flaps. This maneuver made the plane frightfully nose-heavy, so much so that I had to be quick with the elevator trim to relieve pressure on the control column. Otherwise I would have sat there with both arms taut, muscles vibrating, fighting to keep the nose up. After setting the trim, I turned to final approach. Here, again, the weight of the plane, or maybe the lightweight of my P-38 experience, caused me to make another error.

I was used to establishing a landing glide in lighter planes, at slower speeds. As a result, I didn't hold sufficient throttle to maintain 130 mph on final approach. This being my first landing in a P-38, I was preoccupied with other aspects of cockpit management. Suddenly I looked out and I was only 100 feet off the ground and nowhere near the end of the runway. I got on the throttles and held my altitude until I reached the field. I actually made a smooth landing, but it didn't look good with that sloppy, dangerously low approach. If one of those Allisons had coughed and died, when I rapidly applied power to drag the plane in, it would have flipped over and I would never have made it.

A good lesson learned is one you never forget and that was a good lesson. It was through small experiences like that one that flying experience is built, bit by bit. I went to bed that night both happier and smarter than I had gotten up that morning.

After the first flight we went up a few more times to familiarize ourselves with all of our basic flight maneuvers as they were performed in the P-38. It wasn't long before we were flying formation in groups of four. That was indeed great sport!

Flying formation required that we maintain focused attention. For example, if we were in flying four plane right echelon, turning left (away from the echelon) was not hard: trailing planes turned left behind the plane just ahead and to its left, rising slightly and turning on a slightly larger radius, then folding back behind the leader at the same altitude.

But if a right echelon formation turned right (that is, into the trailing echelon) it was more challenging. The trailing planes had to compensate for their shorter turning radii. Before they could turn to follow the leader, they had to slide a little left and a drop a little lower, with the number two plane then quickly banking right to fall in behind leader. The remaining two planes then continued their slides left and lower, with the number three plane banking right and falling in behind number two. And so on for number four, behind number three. Eventually, though, we mastered it and it became a smooth operation for us.

While we were learning, the instructor flew the lead plane and warned us when he was planning to turn. But in time the warnings ceased and we had to maintain an extremely sharp lookout to stay in formation. Our final 20 hours of our pre-graduation flights were all done in P-38s in various formation maneuvers.

On our last flight the instructor flew us north to the Grand Canyon. What a ride! He dropped us into the Canyon and we stayed inside the Canyon for two hours, banking and turning around the Canyon's rock formations.

When we landed back at Williams Field the instructor summoned us to the flight room and informed us that we had completed our last flights as cadets. Our next flight would be as second lieutenants at Fighter Training School in Ontario, California. You can imagine the excitement that greeted that announcement.

The following Sunday we were presented Silver Wings in an impressive ceremony that included Chinese and

Second Lieutenant Schmidt, November 1, 1943.

English pilots that had been in training at their own, nearby flight schools. That ceremony took place on November 1, 1943, my 21st birthday. Following that ceremony, we were given a two-week leave.

Ontario, California

It was a happy time for me in back in Lebanon. I could see the pride in my father's eyes and that meant a great deal to me. I had always been proud of my family and it was good to see them proud of me.

There wasn't a lot to do socially in Lebanon at that time. My friends were all in the service and since I had been away most of the last two years, I wasn't well acquainted with local nightlife. Time slipped by quickly though and soon we were driving me to Albany to catch *The Shasta Daylight* to Los Angeles. But I was a different person boarding that train this time. I was almost a year older, quite a bit wiser (so I thought), and confidently looking forward to the future.

On November 15, 1943, I arrived at Ontario Army Airfield for the first phase of fighter training. The training here was different than we were used to. As cadets, we were accustomed to following orders, doing what we were told, regardless of what we thought of the order or order giver. Now we were commissioned officers and, by act of Congress, considered "gentlemen." Being second lieutenants, we answered only to first lieutenants, captains, majors, colonels and generals, and there weren't too many of them.

We were assigned to Officers Quarters, which meant private rooms, or nearly private since there were four officers in the same room. Finally, I didn't feel like I was sleeping in a train station. Soon the four of us were good friends and close companions, sharing the same thrills, same doubts, same fears, same frustrations; there was no lack of things to talk about. As commissioned officers there was no KP, no latrine duty, no calisthenics. And, best of all, our pay went from $75.00 per month to $220.00 per month. No more standing in line to get a pass for town, either, since the officers could come and go as they pleased as long as they showed up bright-eyed and bushytailed for our next class.

The focus of flight training now became more serious. We were about to learn how to lay waste to everything the enemy had, in the air and on the ground. The first two weeks, the emphasis was on tight formation flying, especially close to the ground. I learned that you hadn't lived till you were the fourth man in a four-plane echelon, 50 feet off the ground at 250 mph, when the leader snapped a turn without warning. If he turned away from the echelon, no problem, duck soup simple, but if he turned toward the echelon, three of us had to quickly slide under one another and bank into the turn one after another. Each plane had to lose a few feet of precious altitude to make its turn and remain in formation. If you were the number four plane there wasn't much altitude left.

It was a wake up call to have to decide whether to touch your buddy's wing, plow up a little Southern California real estate, or thread the needle between. Somehow we managed it. You learned to watch only the flight formation; you didn't look at the ground, you didn't look at anything but your formation leader. You learned to trust your leader; he didn't want to hit California at 250 mph either.

We all got used to low-level formation flight. When he had extra time our flight leader would play follow the leader with us, and we followed him, one behind the other. He flew off into nearby desert and mountains trying to find ways to drop us. Flying under high voltage wires was one of his favorite tricks. You can't see wires at 250 mph, so you had to follow the leader. This was all great fun; I learned a good deal about low-level combat flight this way.

We next took up night training. We took-off in our formation, four at a time about an hour before dark, flew in formation for one to two hours, then split up, climbed to an assigned altitude, flew for another hour, then came in to land one at a time. Ontario's runway was lit along both sides and this made the approach much easier than we had experienced in Basic Flight School. Night landings weren't much more difficult than day landings, the main difference being a shallower final approach to the runway. This allowed more time to correct errors in pitch or yaw. At this lower angle of attack, you flew down to the runway at your normal landing speed, chopped the throttle and you were on the ground.

After we had a few night landings under our belt, we started flying more and more at night. Ontario was about 40 miles east of Los Angeles, so the ground was pretty well lit up even in 1943. There were Navy and Marine flight training centers nearby, so there were many airplanes in the airspace. We used to chase each other around at night, trying to get on to each other's tail. It was good combat practice and a fine way to spend an evening.

We also learned to take-off and land at night, in formation. One night I received an awful fright while landing in formation. The instructors were adamant about keeping the time in the landing pattern to a minimum. Combat aircraft were most vulnerable when landing and taking off, so much emphasis was placed on getting all four planes up or down as quickly as possible. Our landing objective was to have all four planes land simultaneously. They wanted the fourth plane on the runway before the first one finished its landing roll. Everything had to happen quite rapidly and in a coordinated fashion for this to occur.

The landing procedure is started with a low formation pass over the field at around 250 miles per hour. The formation planes then turned left in a climbing turn one at a time, the leader turning at the start of the runway, the second man a third of the way down the runway, the third man two-thirds of the way down and the fourth man at the runway's end. At the apex of the climbing turn, we lowered the landing gear and flaps, frantically spun the elevator trim wheel to lower the nose and initiated a tight descending turn to the approach end of the runway. It made for jolly good fun, but the first night I did it, I was the number four plane. By the time I was turning over the approach end of the runway for my landing there was considerable "dirty air" from the prop wash of the three 38s head of me. That prop wash caught me about 50 feet off the ground, still in my banked turn and nearly flipped my plane upside down. It must have been God and my adrenalin that stabbed that right rudder and slammed the control column right and forward because that P-38 leveled out and hit the runway at the same instant.

I was not proud of one flying incident, especially being a former farm boy. It is something I never related to anyone. It happened during my free time flight near the start of Fighter School. I flew north from Ontario, over a mountain range to another desert to have a look around. While I was out there I spotted a large ranch near mountain's edge. For some reason, I decided to buzz the ranch, not thinking about how scared animals could get. I dove on the ranch, a chicken ranch, and passed over it 20 feet off the ground at 400 mph. I could see chickens running everywhere, but didn't give it much thought.

The next morning there was a notice on the squadron bulletin board, which read as follows:

THIS MORNING UNCLE SAM PAID FOR 213
DEAD CHICKENS. ANY ONE CAUGHT NORTH
OF THE MOUNTAINS NEAR THE ONTARIO AIR
BASE WILL BE OUT. PERIOD.

As you can guess, I never mentioned it to anyone and thankfully no one identified me. Such was war on the home front, as they used to be fond of saying.

I got such a kick out of firing the single 30-caliber gun on the AT-6 that I looked forward to gunnery training on the P-38, with its four 50-caliber guns mounted in the nose of the cockpit nacelle. With those four guns firing at once, the bullets came out in a steady stream like water out of a hose. During our first phase of gunnery practice, we fired only on ground targets. I used what I had learned at flying the AT-6 in Ajo: keep your plane steady, fly at the target until you think you'll crash into it and then squeeze off a few rounds. If you were on target, fire until just before you *know* you'll crash into it, then pull away. If you weren't on target, "walk" the guns into the target with your rudder and repeat the above. The thrill of these fighter exercises made me glad I was alive! With all four of the P-38s guns firing simultaneously, you could actually feel the airplane slow down.

After three weeks, we had completed the first phase of fighter training. There were all kinds of rumors as to where we might go next for Advanced Fighter School, but no one knew. We checked our flight room bulletin board three or four times a day, since that bulletin board was how they communicated with the entire squadron.

Finally, in early December, the order came down and it called for our squadron to split, with half of us remaining at Williams Field and half going to Ellensburg, Washington, on December 16. Being from the Pacific Northwest, I knew how cold Eastern Washington winters could get and I was not anxious to go to Ellensburg. They posted sign-up sheets, one for each location, so we could put in for one or the other assignment. Of course, everyone enjoyed that California sunshine and clear skies, so the Ontario sheet filled almost immediately! That meant the late signers got no choice but Ellensburg, like it or not. There was a lot of pissing and moaning by the late signers. It was rather comical at the time. Half the squadron was on cloud nine, while you would have thought the other half had lost their mothers.

The next day one of the pilots who was going to be married returned to base and discovered where he was going to advanced training: Ellensburg. I knew him pretty well and he knew I was from Oregon. Right away he started working on me about trading lists. He argued that his fiancé couldn't leave California because of her job, so he wouldn't be able to get married, and that I would be able to stop to see family on the way up to Ellensburg, which was all true. He kept after me all evening long and I – being the nice guy that he said I was – finally traded bases with him.

I didn't know it then, but that decision changed my flying career. It meant that I would not become a fighter pilot. In fact, that decision may have saved my life because fighter pilot survival rates during World War II weren't too high.

Ellensburg, Washington

A bitter arctic storm hit Ellensburg just before we arrived that December. It was so cold that we ran to cross the Main Street when going from one bar to the next. I had never been so cold! In the two weeks we were in Ellensburg, we never saw blue sky and we never got off the ground.

It was one evening about Christmas time that our Commanding Officer called a pilots meeting.

"Men," he began, "the word has just come down from Washington that they need more reconnaissance pilots. You men are to report immediately to Will Rogers Field in Oklahoma City for training as photo-recon pilots."

Of course we were keenly disappointed, even crushed,

to hear these words. It was a sad lot of flyboys that filed on to that bus to Will Rogers Field the next day.

But after I learned more about photo-reconnaissance flying, I wasn't so disappointed. It might not be a bad deal: we would fly a fast P-38, no guns, no armor, nothing but the pilot and the cameras. We would fly alone, less likely to attract enemy attention and more dependent on our own wits. Being an independent guy, I liked that and I decided I was going to give it my best shot. Photo shot, that is, not gun shot.

1944
Flying for the 34th PRS

Oklahoma City, Oklahoma

We arrived in Will Rogers Field at the end of December 1943, and started photo-recon training the next day. Navigation was stressed, with major emphasis on dead reckoning. A typical training day consisted of reporting to the flight-ready room at 8:00 a.m. to check the flight board for your assigned practice mission. The flight board was a 20-foot aeronautical chart of the US, with concentric rings drawn at 100-mile intervals from Will Rogers Field. On this map, your mission targets were identified by colored pins and encircled by black grease pencil. You might find as many as seven or eight separate targets, with targets such as airports, reservoirs, rail terminals, or perhaps only latitude and longitude coordinates.

The idea was to develop our skills at finding targets and photographing them from various altitudes, at specified times of day. The targets would be in the same general area, but scattered within a 100-mile radius. Often they were far away; we routinely flew to targets around

New Orleans or Chicago as well as closer targets around Albuquerque or Dallas-Ft. Worth. Mission flights could last four to five hours and a few times even longer.

After we picked up our assignment, we computed our mission flight plan using dead reckoning navigation. We also had to consider the time of day the photos were to be taken, because that determined when we needed to take-off. It was complicated and generally consumed about an hour or so to come up with the flight plan, including all the course headings and estimated times of arrival for each target. We didn't concern ourselves with weather as long as there was a reasonable chance of getting pictures at the target.

Once we completed flight planning, we copied the navigation data on a small clipboard, strapped it to our right thigh, grabbed aeronautical charts for the area and we were off "into the wild blue yonder," as the saying went. As an example, if my first checkpoint was Kansas City and I calculated that flying a heading of 25° for 45 minutes would position me over Kansas City, I would note the time I actually reached Kansas City. I then compared the actual flight time to my calculated flight time. If the two times were close, my flight calculations were confirmed and I continued. But, if they were not, I had to recalculate future checkpoints, correcting for the error I noted between my estimated and my actual flight times to Kansas City.

The Army furnished E6B aviation computers (basically, a circular, aeronautical slide rule) to help with these calculations. The E6B was a fine tool on the ground, but I found it distracting to use when flying so I didn't use it in the air. I would note how far off I was and estimate an adjusted course heading and time to the next target or checkpoint.

Our photo-recon P-38s were equipped with one 24" focal length camera shooting straight down and two 36" cameras shooting obliquely to either side. The cameras were mounted in the nose of the cockpit nacelle where the machine guns were mounted in the fighter version of the P-38. A camera control device, the intervalometer, was located low, between the pilot's legs. With the intervalometer, the pilot could set the intervals between camera shots. The Army liked 60% overlap on a sequential track of photographs, with 40% overlap on side-by-side tracks. The resulting images could then be viewed stereoscopically and appear in 3-D to the photo intelligence analysts.

From 30,000 feet a photograph could cover a lot of territory, so by setting the intervalometer at five to seven seconds we generally recorded the target quite well. After setting the intervalometer, the pilot had only to fly directly over the target, on a precise track over the ground, shooting photographs every few seconds. Obviously, to fly such a ground track required compensating for the wind at the flight altitude. There was also a trigger on the control column that the pilot could use to override intervalometer and take a photograph anytime he wanted, even if the intervalometer were active.

When you were flying straight and level in the P-38 you couldn't see below you very well. The wings and engine booms hid at least a 20 square mile area directly underneath you. This fact complicated target photography. No one ever told me the best way to assure I got the target photographs, so I developed my own system. I approached the target at a 45° angle to the desired photo track. As I arrived over the desired track, I banked 90° to look straight down and check my position accuracy, then immediately leveled the wings and started shooting. Most of the time I clicked off a few extra photos with the override switch when I judged myself to be dead on the target.

After twelve weeks, we completed the photo-recon training and prepared to leave for combat. We left Oklahoma City in April for Shreveport for altitude decompression checks. The Army wanted every combat pilot to pass a decompression test before going overseas. At a base in Shreveport, there was a decompression chamber, a huge tank with room enough for six people to sit on each side. We went inside, donned oxygen masks and they quickly pumped air out of the chamber until the air pressure inside was equivalent to an altitude of 30,000 feet. They wanted to see if any of us developed sudden pain in the ear canals. The pain was impossible to hide due to its severity. At the first sign of discomfort to anyone they stopped the test and returned slowly to normal atmospheric pressure. Fortunately, I passed, but around three percent of the pilots failed it. I never learned what happened to those pilots; I assumed they made them flight instructor or ferry pilots.

Deployment

From Shreveport, we went to Savannah to be outfitted for combat. We wanted to get to Savannah because we could tell by the weight of the uniforms they issued to us whether we were headed for Europe or the Pacific. I wanted to go to Europe, so I was relieved to be handed the heavier uniforms.

From Savannah, we went to Camp Kilmer, New Jersey, twenty miles south New York City. Camp Kilmer was the New York Port of Embarkation for Army forces bound for the European Theatre of Operations. It was a giant staging area for servicemen.

At Kilmer we were assigned to a combat unit. I was assigned to the 34th Photo-Reconnaissance Squadron (34th PRS) stationed at Chalgrove Airfield, near Oxford, England. The 34th PRS had begun operations at Chalgrove as a new squadron only two months before. During early photo-recon deployment planning, the 34th PRS had been slated for service in Italy, but

My passport photo, before de-parting for England, May 1944.

through a twist of fate the Commanding Officers of the newly created 32nd and 34th PRS flipped a coin to see which squadron went to England and which to Italy. The 34th

PRS got England, so on March 21, 1944 all the men of the 34th PRS departed Camp Kilmer for Chalgrove. A few weeks later, the men of the 32nd PRS left for Italy on the liberty ship *SS Paul Hamilton*. On April 20, off the coast of Gibraltar, a German submarine torpedoed and sank the *Paul Hamilton*, with a loss of all souls.

At Camp Kilmer, I ran into two other photo-recon pilots also bound for the 34th. In early May, the 34th lost three pilots in low-level reconnaissance runs over the beaches of Normandy, the soon to be D-day invasion beaches. We three were headed over to replace those pilots.

On May 20, 1944 we got the word to pack up, we were leaving. We took the short ride on a troop train from Kilmer into New York City, where 2,500 of us formed columns of four and marched from the train station to Pier 59. As we marched to the pier, we could see a large, fine looking French ship, the *Ile de France*, moored to the right of Pier 59. On the left side of the pier, was moored a smaller, foul-smelling ship, the *HMS Rangitata*.

We marched on to the pier and stood there, at attention, facing out the pier toward the Hudson River. We desperately hoped to hear the command: "Right face!" We waited for what seemed like five minutes before the sergeant barked: "Left face!" Twenty-five hundred jaws dropped as we turned and boarded the *Rangitata* for Liverpool. By 1944, the *Rangitata* had already been a troop transport for three years. And it looked like it. The top deck was lined with open garbage cans that, I was sure, had never been washed. The garbage cans were necessary because garbage was never tossed overboard for the German U-boats to find and follow. With troops billeted below deck, there was no place but the upper deck for stowing garbage.

With 2,533 men on a ship built for 580 passengers things were crowded. As officers, we were lucky, we got staterooms. The enlisted men slept barracks-style in the hold. I didn't see their sleeping arrangements, but we officers were assigned 10 to 20 to staterooms originally intended for two or four. This was accomplished by stacking bunks five high, the bottom bunk being on the floor and the top bunk being 18 inches below the ceiling. There was just barely enough room to sleep. If you wanted to read in bed you had to turn on your side to do it.

Crossing the Atlantic

Most of the troops acquired a queasy stomach by the time we reached the open sea. For the first two days, it was hard to find an empty place at the rail.

The *Rangitata* was 550 feet long, so in rough seas the ship pitched decidedly fore and aft in rhythm with the swells. The bow or stern alternately rose or plunged as the ship moved through the swell or trough. During a part of this cycle the stern was often lifted clear of the sea and the propeller would spin in the air for a few seconds. Every time this happened, the propeller shaft and bearings vibrated loudly throughout the aft of the ship. Since the sea was rough for most of the crossing, this was the typical state of affairs. Unfortunately, I knew this too well because I was in a third-deck stateroom, directly over the

HMS Rangitata, as a passenger ship, ca. 1930.

shaft.

We were part of a convoy of 45 ships. There were four escort carriers, not much larger that our *Rangitata*. Their decks were filled with airplanes, lashed down against the heavy North Atlantic seas. Then there were the many tankers, freighters and troop ships. In our pre-boarding briefing, we were told not to worry about being torpedoed because the troop ships would be placed at the interior of the convoy.

The convoy captains evidently had not heard this briefing, because the escort carriers were placed most safely in the convoy's center, surrounded next by fuel tankers, then the freighters and finally the troop ships around the outer edge. The only ships beyond us were the small destroyer escorts, around 300 feet in length, that patrolled the areas outside of the convoy with sonar, radar, and lookouts, monitoring for German submarines. These destroyer escorts were tossed around even more than the *Rangitata*. I watched their masts swinging at 45° from vertical most of the crossing. It was a mystery to me how they cooked meals under those conditions.

The tankers moved through the seas very differently. I had doubted their sea-worthiness because they had so little freeboard, only about 10 feet. There was a small superstructure on either end that stuck up another 25 feet or so, but most of the ship was only barely above the sea. The large swells that caused us the pitch fore and aft seemed only to raise and lower the entire tanker. On its downward cycle, a tanker went almost out of sight. I could have believed it was sinking. But after a time, up it would bob. The full up-down cycle took about a minute. From our vantage point in the convoy, we could see usually see about five tankers, two escort carriers and one destroyer.

There wasn't much to do to pass the time on board. I spent a lot of time either on the bow watching the phosphorescence in the bow wake or on the aft deck watching the phosphorescence in the propeller turbulence. I watched that turbulence, noting the similarity with the air disturbed by the aircraft propeller. With the sea, though, you could clearly visualize the disturbance. I also spent a good amount of time reading. The Army furnished us with books, printed about half the size of a regular book. These were current novels, covering a wide variety of interests.

About a week out of New York, we entered the submarine danger zone and were told to wear life jackets all the time. We were issued a small red light, powered by a single D cell battery. This was to be turned on in the event that the ship went down, to make it easier for searchers to find survivors. The lights were almost worthless, though, as half of them didn't work when we tried activating them on the ship. Still, we wore them as directed.

It was the next morning that I experienced my first war scare. The incident showed how jumpy we were all getting now that we were in an area where we could meet an untimely and unexpected end. I had seen large guns mounted fore and aft on the *Rangitata*, but they were never manned and I paid no attention to them. One morning early, around 5:00, I awoke to sudden, loud bang! The ship shuddered and shook. Without even thinking, I raced up three decks and stood at the rail, ready to abandon ship. I thought we had been torpedoed! And, if the ship was going to sink, I wanted off. I wasn't the only one worried about this, because within seconds the rail was five deep in troops ready to go over the side.

The gunners hadn't warned us that they routinely cleared the guns upon entering a submarine danger zone. None of us Army guys had ever heard a large gun go off. It was such a relief to learn it was a false alarm that we didn't mind the scare.

We zigzagged across the North Atlantic for 10 days. By then, I was glad I was in the Air Corps and not the Navy. Finally, when we were 12 hours out from Liverpool, the convoy broke up and every shipped raced to port at their own top speed.

Maybe now, I hoped we could pull away from the slower vessels (because convoys only travel at the top cruising speed of its slowest ship). And, before long we were alone, behind every other convoy vessel then steaming ahead of us.

Liverpool was another gigantic staging area similar to Camp Kilmer. It took a few days for everyone to be processed and sent on to their respective organizations. We three 34ᵗʰ PRS pilots eventually found ourselves on a train to join our squadron at Chalgrove Airfield.

Chalgrove Airfield/High Wycombe, England

We got to Chalgrove on June 7, 1944, the day after the D-day invasion. We went immediately to the commander's office to introduce ourselves. As we entered his office, the CO, Colonel Don Hayes, sat at his desk, scanning our flight resumes. He looked up as we entered, greeted us and motioned for us to take a seat on an old couch against the wall.

"You know, boys, when I received your resumes, thought that the War Department had a mixed up and sent me three Luftwaffe pilots. You'll have to admit the names on this roster are highly unusual: Schmidt, Von Tempsky and Walters. But as long as Uncle Sam vouches for you, I'll take you on. Go over to the supply sergeant to pick up your flying gear and a bicycle. You're going to need a bicycle; this is an awfully large base." I didn't learn until 20 years later that the entire British Intelligence was located beneath that air base.

Col. Don Hayes, 34ᵗʰ PRS, 1944. Photo courtesy of 34ᵗʰ PRS Association.

The three of us then headed to our squadron's Quonset

hut, stowed our personal gear and met the other pilots. They were a friendly bunch and it wasn't long before we felt at home. The hut had a wood stove, but it didn't put out much heat. It was cool and the weather was poor all summer, even into August when we finally left Chalgrove to reposition our operations near Rennes, France. It rained at least some everyday we were there.

Our 8th Air Force headquarters was located a few miles southeast of Chalgrove, at High Wycombe. This area was 11 miles southeast of Oxford and 40 northwest of London. It had a remarkable pastoral beauty, with gently rolling countryside, quaint English villages, and now and then a small river with a picturesque stone-arched bridge. The Thames ran through the area. The villages along its banks all had little harbors to shelter the boats that plied that famous river.

Before we new pilots were released to fly combat missions, we were taken on local flights to familiarize ourselves with the area. It was on one of these orientation flights that I first experienced aviator's vertigo. I had read about spatial disorientation and vertigo, but living it was a stronger lesson and this incident got my attention.

I took-off in a flight of four P-38s; I was the last plane in a four-plane echelon formation. There was a low overcast so we flew into clouds and instrument conditions from the start of the flight. While climbing out, I could barely see the number three plane, just in front of me and to my left, let alone the whole formation. At about 18,000 feet, it seemed to me that the formation abruptly left me, executing a sharp climbing turn to the left; I was alone in the clouds.

What actually happened was that I turned right and slipped into a spiraling dive. I was so sure they had left me, climbing to the left, that it never occurred to me that I was a victim of vertigo. However, I soon learned the truth of the matter as I came out of the clouds in a tight downward spiral to the right! The ceiling was low enough that I didn't have much altitude to recover. Reacting instantly, I leveled the wings and pulled back as hard as I could on the control column. I recovered so close to the ground that I saw individual needles on the fir trees. It was one of those flying moments when I was very glad to be alive.

What I thought might have caused this incident was flying formation in clouds. I had never done this (and I never did it again). When flying in formation you don't watch your instruments, you just do what is necessary with flight controls and power to stay in position with the formation. As the fourth man, with my only reference point being the wing of the plane ahead of me, not looking at my instruments resulted in a classic case of aviator's vertigo. I had learned a good lesson and after that I was highly alert to risk of vertigo.

On the next day, June 14, 1944, I reported to the Flight Ready Room for my first combat mission. I was assigned to fly cover for a more experienced pilot on a mapping run of the southern part of the Brest peninsula. I was quite excited as this was my first mission and I wanted to do well. On the way to the area we were to photograph, we flew over the city of Brest and the German anti-aircraft guns opened up on us. Soon, we were flying through a layer of smoke and flak. When anti-aircraft shells explode they form a large, dark area due to the powder burned. This much you see easily, but the flying shrapnel are small and move fast so they are invisible. Although I had known for a year and a half that this was going to be a hazardous occupation, it really sank in as I saw all the shells the Germans were throwing at two airplanes.

It was a shock the first time I was shot at. But it never bothered me much after that, except for my tendency to close my eyes if the shell exploded close to me. We were to maintain radio silence over enemy territory, but we always left our radio receivers on to listen. The British had

After returning from my first mission.

good radar and they kept good track of the enemy planes. The first time I heard a voice on the radio sing out, "There is a report of fifty bandits over Paris," and I was only ten miles from Paris, you never saw an airplane turn so fast in your life!

After flying cover for three missions, I went out on my own. It was a good feeling: I was responsible only to myself and could fly where and how I wanted as long as I came back with photos of my assigned targets. Our missions at this time were mostly mapping missions over the west coast of France. The Allied Command was trying to mislead the Germans as to where the next Allied attack would come from. We knew the Germans forces paid very close attention to the areas the photo-recon planes flew, believing that these reconnaissance missions were preludes to pending attacks.

The weather was not good over western France that June so most of our missions entailed an hour or more of instrument flight through clouds en route to the targets. Our navigation was all by dead reckoning. We computed these flight plans on the ground, then flew to the target vicinity at 30,000 feet. Often, upon descending from the clouds, I would be surprised how close I was to a target. Sometimes I was within ten miles of it, but nearly always I was within twenty to thirty miles of it, and that was close enough to see it. Our normal squadron guidelines were to shoot the mission's photos at an altitude of 30,000 feet, if it was clear at that level; if it was not clear, then to let down to 20,000 feet and shoot the photos at that level; and if it wasn't clear at 20,000 feet, then we could come home without photos. Pilots, however, had discretion to descend lower, if they were comfortable doing so, to find an altitude at which they could get photos. I always descended to a level where I could get clear photos. I couldn't see risking a good plane and a good (I hoped) pilot on a long flight over enemy territory and then coming back empty-handed.

If we photographed 75% of our target areas, usually from 10 to 12 per mission, except when we were doing mapping runs, it was counted as a successful mission, or a "blue" mission. Unsuccessful missions were counted as "red" ones. I was up there with the squadron leaders in the "blue" mission category.

We had plenty of time off because all the pilots had to do was fly missions or be in the Flight Ready Room, ready to fly missions, at the assigned times. We played ping-pong and various card games, mostly Hearts and Bridge, to kill time. And, of course, we engaged in lots of horseplay since we were all just out of our teens and full of piss and vinegar.

We had an excellent weatherman in the squadron; he seldom missed a forecast. As long as the visibility exceeded one-half mile and the cloud ceiling was 500 feet or higher, we flew. But if our weatherman said the weather was going to be bad enough to keep planes grounded for a day or two, we liked to take a train into London.

The first time I went to London, I didn't expect much. The city was blacked-out and drab. Sandbags were stacked to shield the fronts of every building. As we walked down one street, though, we began to hear some music. We looked around, trying to identify the source. We found it coming from a doorway between two storefronts. Inside the door, a flight of stairs led up to a public dance hall. As we entered the stairwell, we heard a dance band upstairs playing one of that day's more popular tunes, "The Beer Barrel Polka." Needless to say, we hurried upstairs, paid the ten shillings admittance fee and walked in. It was a large hall, filled with people dancing and having a good time. Some friendly folks invited us over to their table and we had fun there. The British loved to dance, so there were plenty of dance halls in London. There were also good USO centers in London. This experience changed our opinion of wartime England. There may have been in a war, but the British still knew how to have a good time.

As we returned to the airbase after that dance we couldn't believe our good luck: only two hours after we entered a large, foreign city at war, we were having as much fun as we had stateside. We were able to visit London quite a lot. It was about a 40-mile train ride from High Wycombe to London, with a neat little train running between the cities every hour or so. The British trains were small, about half the size of US trains, with shrill whistles. The stations had platforms, elevated to train door level so you didn't have to step up or down like we were used to. The passenger cars had doors on the station side and they all flew open at once upon arrival, making getting on and off quicker and easier. The coaches had several compartments and each compartment held about 10 people. It was a fast and efficient way to move people. We could have learned a lot from their public transportation.

Getting ready for missions required preparation. At 30,000 feet the air is much colder than on the ground, so we wore felt lined boots, a warm jacket and gloves. There were heaters in the P-38, but they weren't effective at that altitude.

In the cockpit, we sat on our survival life raft, a one-man raft with three signal flares, a fold up water bucket and some emergency food. We also carried a small emergency kit in a small, sealed box, one inch thick, and four inches by six inches in size. In this kit we carried a compass, fishing line and hook, four condensed food bars, German money, maps of the area we were flying over, a signal mirror, matches, candles and a knife.

In addition to all of this we carried a 45-caliber Colt handgun in a belt holster. And, of course, we had a parachute. When we sat down in the cockpit we first buckled on our life raft and then the parachute. After getting as comfortable as we could, because the seat was not padded, we fastened the flight harness across our lap

Pre-mission briefing, Chalgrove, 1944.

and over each shoulder. We then put on a leather aviator helmet, which contained a set of radio earphones, our throat mike and finally our oxygen mask. Although oxygen wasn't needed at lower altitudes we always donned our masks on the ground. We checked to insure the mask fit snuggly, the oxygen bottle was full and the pressure was correct. In addition to all this gear we had our flight plan clipboard, with target information, compass courses, checkpoints and times, strapped to our right thigh.

Only then were we ready to crank up the big Allison engines. There was always a mechanic with a fire extinguisher standing by each engine in case of fire. The P-38 had an inertial starter, run by two 12-volt batteries. There wasn't much reserve power in them after starting both engines, so we were careful to start them on the first try. With the fuel-air mixture control levers in the full forward, choke position and the throttle just cracked we would engage the inertial starter. As the flywheel built up speed, the whine increased in pitch until it was almost shrieking. This took about a minute to get the revolutions up to the RPM required for engine start. We could judge that time by the pitch of the flywheel whine. At that moment, we engaged the starter and with any luck the engine would cough, buck and roar to life. Properly adjusting the mixture with a little more air and a little more throttle resulted in an Allison purring like a 1,150 horsepower kitten. With the left engine up, we would repeat the procedure on the right one. When everything looked good, we gave the mechanics the "thumbs up" and they removed the wheel chocks.

At the end of the runway, I would set the brakes hard. This took a lot of foot pressure. Then I opened the engines to full take-off power and ran them for a minute. This was to insure they were running properly because if one quit before you were at flying speed the airplane could flip over rapidly. As the engine power increased, the airplane would shake and groan. When I was ready, releasing the brakes threw me back in the seat as the plane quickly accelerated down the runway. When the airspeed reached 100 mph, I pulled the control column back and flipped the landing gear lever. As I reached safe flying speed, around 170 mph, I raised the flaps slowly, trimmed the controls and set a course for the first leg of the mission.

Flying over to France entailed 100 to 120 miles of flight over the English Channel. For some reason, the airplane's engines always seemed to run rougher over water. But the P-38 had two engines so it wasn't much of a worry. We could only fly to and from France over two specific routes. One was Selsey Bill and the other, Beachy Head. If you were anywhere else over the channel, you would get an escort of British fighters.

As I said earlier, the weather in England was generally bad. Sometimes it worsened while you were away on a mission. One time it had became so bad it took me a half hour and seven tries to find the field before I could land.

It had been a long mission and I was the last pilot to return that day. Visibility was not over one-quarter mile, the ceiling was down to 300 feet and it was raining hard. We had navigation aids but no landing aids of any kind. By calling the field, with a long, 20-second call, they would give us the heading to the field. Then, when they heard you fly over the field they would contact you on the radio. This was all they could do, the rest was up to the pilot. This system worked fine for ceilings around 500 feet above.

I flew over the field, got my radio call, then descended to around 250 ft and tried to find the field. But visibility was poor with the intense rain and I could not find the field. There were no good landmarks near Chalgrove; that part of England all looked like a big golf course from the air, so there was nothing for me to orient myself with. Six times I attempted this routine and six times I failed to see the field. On my seventh try I caught a glimpse of the field as I shot by. I racked the plane into a 90° bank and headed back to the field and set her down. This was the only time I ever kissed the ground after a landing.

My brother, Leo, was also stationed in England at that time, on the coast, south of me. Leo was with the 4th Armored Division of General George Patton's 3rd Army. The 3rd Army didn't take part in D-Day operations, but moved into France, in July 1944 to engineer the breakout at Avranches and subsequently chased the Germans to the Rhine. We had an L-4 liaison plane (a military version of the Piper Cub) in our squadron for general transportation. One day, I got permission to fly down and see Leo.

When I got there I saw so many bombs, gas cans, tanks, trucks and other gear that I wondered what kept England from tipping that way. There wasn't a real airfield there, just a wind sock on a pole in a farm field. The 3rd Army also had a bunch of L-4s, which they used for artillery spotting.

After the visit with Leo, I went to take-off, but found I couldn't get up enough speed to clear the fence at the end of the field. I pondered this problem for a few minutes and decided to put down full flaps, run up to the fence as fast as the L-4 could go, jerk back on the stick and hope the plane would jump up enough to clear the fence before falling back to the adjacent field where I could finish my take-off run. It worked to perfection. I thought I was so inventive to come up with such a maneuver until I got a letter from Leo telling me that this take-off maneuver was a standard operation for their artillery spotters.

One of my high school friends, Jack Tucker, was a member of the 33rd PRS, which was also stationed at Chalgrove Airfield at that time. Jack wasn't a pilot so I used to get the L-4 and take him up for joy rides along the Thames River. We liked to fly up behind the haystacks, where we occasionally broke up a lovers tryst, cutting the engine and gliding silently until we were just above them. We would halloo them out the open window.

Since Jack was in a Photo-Recon squadron like me, it was easy to stay in touch with him throughout the War. I saw him from time to time, flying over in an L-4 when he was stationed nearby, and even flying over in a P-38 when he was stationed farther away.

Photo-recon squadrons were uncommon outfits. We were a self-contained and autonomous unit. With only about 350 men, we knew each other well. Our commanding officer, Colonel Hayes, was always readily available to us. I had no problem getting permission to use squadron aircraft if they were available. As I look back on that situation, I believe this must have been a privilege enjoyed by few other servicemen of my rank.

In the latter part of June I was picked to take on an extensive mapping mission with our executive officer, Major James Dempsey. Major Dempsey was one of two West Point graduates on our flying roster. The Allied Command wanted an up-to-date map of the Rhine River and vicinity from the mouth at the North Sea to the Swiss border.

As this would require more film than one plane could carry, we used two planes. Major Dempsey would photograph the northern segment of the mission and I would shoot the southern segment. Besides getting pictures of all the Rhine bridges and Rhine river barge traffic, we would be taking pictures of all railroad marshalling yards and airports near the Rhine.

These photographs would become the standard used to detect enemy movement of troops, airplanes, or materiel. This was the longest mission I had flown, requiring more than four hours to complete. The weather was good and everything came off according to plan. I was awarded the Distinguished Flying Cross for this mission, one of six won by pilots in our squadron during the War.

On August 5, as I returned to the briefing room after a mission over France's Loire River valley, the operations officer came up to me and informed me that the Allied forces had finally broken out from their limited beachhead in Normandy and now controlled the area around

Cherbourg. He added that he had two generals to ferry to Cherbourg, but the only airport there was so heavily damaged none of our larger planes could get in.

Being awarded the Distinguished Flying Cross, 1944.

He wanted to know if I could ferry the generals over in a light aircraft. These generals were charged with preparing the port of Cherbourg to receive heavy Allied shipments of fuel and war materiel and they needed to be in Cherbourg *yesterday!*

Our squadron had a light, 6-place liaison plane, with short field capability, the Cessna UC-78. The UC-78 was a light, fabric covered aircraft, with wood-framed wings and tail, earning it the dubious nickname: "The Bamboo

Bomber." I had flight experience in the UC-78, so the three of us piled in and I cranked her up. We left so hurriedly that I had to compute my course and estimated time of arrival in the air.

There was a low overcast and the visibility was poor. I didn't want to be wandering over occupied France in this frail machine, so I paid close attention to my navigation. The overcast got even lower over the Channel, so I was soon flying in the clouds, on instruments. Due to the small peninsula that we then controlled, I was limited to a relatively small piece of friendly real estate. I figured my elapsed time should be one hour and fifteen minutes. About an hour and ten minutes into the flight, the clouds thinned and lifted a little. I had been low, flying at 300 feet, hoping this might happen. A few minutes later I spotted the French coastline, orientated myself and landed the generals as planned. I received a short tour around the newly captured territory and was given a German helmet as a souvenir.

The generals were grateful to be there, but probably not half as glad as I was to leave them there. I didn't care much for the ferry pilot business. I flew home just in time for the evening meal. It had been an exciting opportunity; as it turned out, I became the first member of our squadron to walk

Cessna UC-78, "The Bamboo Bomber." Photo courtesy of www.WarbirdAlley.com.

on French soil.

There was a general feeling of elation as the news spread of the Allies breakout and our control of the Cherbourg Peninsula. This was the first big success for Allied forces after two months of close range infantry combat on a narrow strip of the Normandy coast. Cherbourg gave us a port to unload heavy war equipment and sped up materiel transfer, especially fuel.

Bad weather grounded us for the next three days, so we all decided to make one last trip to London. With the success in France, we knew we would soon be repositioned to a base in western France. Having more time, we stayed the night at the Savoy Hotel, down the street from Piccadilly Circus, which is the Times Square of London. We all had the same idea; we were looking for some excitement. Things were pretty lively around Piccadilly, so we visited a few choice pubs before looking for a dance or carnival. A few of us were walking down one street full of apartments and spotted two British beauties looking out a third story window. We gave them a hearty greeting, which they acknowledged with ready smiles.

From this point, though, things went downhill. We had an amusing routine (we thought it was amusing anyway) that we used when we encountered an attractive woman. We would whinny like a horse, paw the ground with our right foot and close with a snort, the way horses do in greeting one another. This was meant as a compliment, as a show of our enthusiasm for the fairer sex.

This time, after spotting a gutter drainpipe leading up

to within a few feet of their window, I bounded up the drainpipe to their level and went into my interested-horse routine. Little did I realize that two Army MPs were nearby, witnessing this scene. As they came walking up, I don't need to tell you that I came down the drain faster than I went up

They confronted me with disgusted looks. The larger and closer MP started, "Lieutenant, what in the world are you doing? As an officer in the US Army, you are a disgrace to that uniform and your service!"

"Your behavior is completely out of line," added the other MP. "You wouldn't act like this at home, would you?"

I replied, "If I did it here, I would do it at home."

"Well, you certainly are NOT going to do it here." The first MP shot back.

"Well," I answered back, "if I wouldn't do it here, I wouldn't do it at home,"

"BUT YOU DID IT HERE," shouted the first MP, who was working up a head of steam.

"Like I said, if I would do it here, I would do it at home."

I don't remember exactly how this Abbott and Costello routine finally ended, but I wound up with a citation. I was lucky to get out of that situation and neighborhood as easily as I did.

Over the course of the rest of the War, I was cited three more times, once when I was home in Lebanon and went to town without my uniform coat. They were all harmless, with no ill will intended to anyone.

A-Flight, 34th Photo Reconnaissance Squadron, July 1944. I am front row, third from left and Phil Hooke, third from right.

Rennes, France

On August 11, our squadron moved to an airfield near Rennes, France, on the Brest peninsula. The field had been captured only two days before and there was still enemy activity nearby. We were ordered to dig a slit trench to jump into in the event of enemy action. I dug my trench in my tent and put my cot over it so if the Germans started shooting, all I had to do was fall into it. I never had to use it, but it gave me a comfortable feeling to know it was there.

The day after we set up operations in Rennes, a Ju 52 German transport (similar to a DC-3) attempted to land there. He obviously was not aware that the airfield was no longer in German hands. The German pilot must have noticed the P-38s on the flight line just as he touched down, because he immediately gunned his engines to take-off for friendlier skies. We had installed 12 anti-aircraft guns, six on each side of the field, but believe it or not, not a shot was fired at him! He dipped his wing in recognition as he flew away. I imagined fur flew in our squadron's anti-aircraft section that night.

The Germans had left an arms depot next to the field at Rennes. Due to the flux of a battlefield, it was completely unguarded when we arrived. This was during the time that General Patton's Army was chasing the Germans madly across France and the Allied troops had already moved on after the Germans and the rear echelon troops hadn't arrived yet so we had complete run of the arms depot. The depot contained munitions of every size and description, a variety of grenades, smoke canisters, and artillery shells, large and small. To us Air Corps flyboys, this was just like a candy store of firecrackers and souvenirs there for the taking. And we took a lot and we got into some trouble for it, as well.

The first bit of trouble started innocently. We "liberated" a few cases of smoke canisters and began igniting them. They spewed colored smoke. We threw the canisters around outside to watch the vivid yellow, green, red or blue smoke. The bad thing about them was that their smoke stuck to anything it came in contact with.

Our camp was set up in two rows of Army pyramid tents. Some genius came up idea of throwing canisters into the tents of another squadron based there at the airfield. This was all it took to start a smoke canister war. Before long, almost every tent on the base was one color or another, inside and out. Eventually this escalated to where someone made the mistake of throwing a canister into the CO's tent. This did not go over well, not at all. His tent may have been yellow inside, but his language was blue outside as he vented his anger on us. He lined us up at attention and we stood there for two hours.

The next day though, we went back to the ammo dump, this time picking through cases of hand grenades. There was a canal running through this area with locks on it. The locks were hand-operated, by the boatmen who plied the canal. We threw a grenade into some shallow water and were rewarded with a satisfactory KABOOM! and a 40 foot geyser. It wasn't long before a grenade landed in deeper water. This made a deep WHUMP! sound, with a big water fountain and killed a lot of fish.

We killed hundreds of little ones and two or three big ones with every grenade. We gathered up the big ones and traded them to a farmer for eggs.

Tiring of this disgusting pastime, we decided to experiment and see how close we could get to grenade explosions. There were hundreds of bomb craters around the airfield as Allied bombers tried to interdict traffic by blowing up canal bridges. First, we crouched in one crater and threw a grenade into a crater three or four craters away. But as this game progressed, we threw them into closer and closer craters until we were throwing them into adjacent craters. This pastime was entertaining enough until a tree branch an inch and a half thick and just above our heads disappeared in a grenade blast. That stopped our grenade-in-the-crater game rather suddenly.

Everyone wanted souvenirs from the ammo dump, but the munitions were all live, fused and ready to fire. As such, no one could use them for souvenirs. In visiting with an infantryman in the area one day I mentioned this and he explained to me how to take shells apart and remove fuses from the grenades. So with this newfound knowledge, I went back to the dump and picked up some German potato-masher grenades, 50-caliber shells, 20-mm cannon shells, and a few incendiary bombs. I took them out to the middle of an empty field to defuse. As I did this, everyone else retreated to the edges of the field. They wanted souvenirs, too, but they evidently didn't have much confidence in my defusing ability. The 20-mm shell presented a challenge in that the middle set of three threads required to unscrew the fuse was a left-hand thread. Pressure applied in the wrong direction would have been extremely dangerous.

I worked at this, alone, in the field, for an hour or so and came away with some nice trophies. Two days later our squadron's dentist tried the same thing and blew out one eye and two fingers on his right hand. Twenty minutes after that incident, a guard detail was stationed on the ammo dump.

Another way we occupied ourselves at Rennes, was swimming in a nearby rock quarry. A raft floated in the middle of the quarry pool and we kept a bar of soap on it so we could bathe whenever we went swimming. While walking along the quarry bank to go swimming one day, on an impulse, I pulled my 45-caliber Colt pistol out of its holster and told everybody to watch the bar of soap on the raft. The pool level was a good 30 feet below ground level and the raft was some distance from shore, so the bar of soap was far away to expect to hit it with a handgun. But I raised my pistol and without taking aim, pointed and fired. Surprisingly, the bar of soap exploded with my shot. We replaced the bar so everyone could try their luck at it. We shot at that second bar of soap all afternoon and no one hit it, though we shot the raft to pieces.

Reading this you might get the idea we did little more than play, but that would be far from the truth. We were extremely busy trying to keep up with the 3rd Army's requests for up-to-date intelligence. Our squadron pilots were flying everyday during available photo-hours. In Photo-Recon, available photo-hours meant from about 9:30 a.m. to 4:30 p.m. Any earlier or later and there were too many shadows on the targets. In my 10 days at Rennes, I flew five combat missions.

Chateaudun, France

It was during this time, August 1944, that the 3rd Army was chasing the German forces across France. With the 3rd Army moving, we were too. We soon got orders to reposition the 34th to Chateaudun, 40 miles southeast of Paris. We arrived in Chateaudun on August 23.

Chateaudun had been a major French airbase before the War, with an excellent concrete runway. The Germans improved the field during their time there, but Allied bombing had since destroyed it, leaving many craters. As we moved in, a construction battalion was there working on the field. They filled in the runway craters and we went to work.

Two days after we got to Chateaudun, Paris was liberated. Our squadron's commander and executive officer planned a trip into Paris to find some equipment our squadron needed. They ask Phil Hooke, a pilot friend, and me, to go with them. It was an exciting trip for us.

The Parisians were delirious over being freed from four years of German occupation. From the

Me with Phil Hooke in Paris, 1944.

attention they gave us, they must have thought that we were the ones that freed them.

From Chateaudun we flew daily mapping missions over our sector of the front. We photographed the battlefront and 15 miles into enemy territory. We also photographed every airfield and marshalling yard in the sector. These mapping flights were new tasks, over and above our regular target intelligence missions so our workload was building. By then we were receiving new planes and new pilots on a sustained basis.

New planes went to the next pilot in seniority that didn't already have a plane with his name on it. It was about this time that I became the most senior pilot without an assigned plane, so the next new P-38 to be ferried in would be mine.

It was a beauty: one of the new F-5E series of photo-

Strato Snob and me, 30 miles southwest of Paris, August 1944.

recon P-38s, the first one in our squadron. The new F-5Es had aileron boost for faster turns and combat dive flaps for reduced turning radius and steeper dives. It was painted sky blue on the bottom and dark blue on the top. My crew chief, "Red" Smith, wasted no time getting his and my name on its nose. I let the mechanics pick out the name and symbol for it. They named it *Strato Snob*. Having your own plane meant that if you were flying, you had priority to use that aircraft.

One Sunday I went up in one of our older P-38s to put some "slow time" on its replacement engines. We always gave replacement engines four hours of flight time before we considered them to be combat ready. Coming back in to land that afternoon, I made a decision I later regretted.

As I flew over the field, I could see that it was lined with French civilians from Chateaudun, having a look-see

Crew Chief "Red" Smith with our Strato Snob, 1944.

at all the Allied equipment. Across from the field from the French, there was a POW holding area filled with new German POWs just up from the south of France. Having such a large audience for a landing must have addled my brain because I decided to show off a little and let them see just how hot this American pilot was.

The hotter the pilot – so we thought – the closer you touched down to the end of the runway and the shorter your landing roll. I planned to bring it in slow, barely above its 110 mph stall speed, and chop the power the second I crossed the runway threshold, touching down on the very end of the runway. However, I happened to be flying a well-used and battered bird that stalled at 115 mph. So about 40 feet in the air and still 50 feet short of the threshold, the plane stalled, nosed over and, like so much heavy metal, fell to the earth.

Wallace Bosworth (left), Neil Walters (back) and me, August 1944.

Luckily, I was low enough that the plane hit at 45°, bounced and landed on the runway end with enough forward momentum to allow me to steer it off of the runway. When it stopped in the grass, the main landing gear struts were driven up through the engine booms and both propellers were bent. I cut the switches, jumped out and ran away as fast as I could, but it didn't blow up.

The German POWs let out a big yell and clapped their hands. My fellow pilots thought it no less hilarious, especially because they knew I had been trying to show off. As I walked over to the flight line, one of my cohorts yelled, "Hey, Larry, four more planes and you'll be a German Ace!" It was one of my most embarrassing moments.

I reported what I had done to the CO. He never said a cross word, but told me to write home to tell my folks to buy more War Bonds. He came around his desk, patted me on the back and said, "Take up another one up and let me see you make a good landing." That experience removed any desire on my part to attempt foolish flying stunts.

Saint-Dizier, France

As we were getting things organized in our temporary home in Chateaudun, we were ordered again to move nearer our 3rd Army HQ. On September 12, we left Chateaudun for Saint-Dizier, about 150 miles farther east. Saint-Dizier was a major Allied base and we expected to be there for some time. We were told to winterize our camp so we installed wooden floors in our tents, raising them three feet off the ground. There was a German stove factory nearby so every tent got a new German stove.

The American 7th Army had driven up from the south of France and was now in position between the 3rd Army and France's 1st Army. We now had three armies to provide photo-reconnaissance for. This workload kept us busy and out of trouble.

When I returned from a mission, I usually let down after crossing into friendly territory and flew 40 feet off the ground along the major roads in that area until I was near our airbase. One day I mistook one of the rivers in the area and let down still about 50 miles inside enemy territory. I was leisurely flying along at only 200 mph when it suddenly felt like I flew over an erupting volcano. I had flown up to the battlefront from the German side, at a low speed, on a straight, predictable course. I had never seen so many guns firing! It was amazing how the enemy could get so many guns into play in such a short span of time. Although I flew through this curtain of fire, they never touched me. It is hard to hit an airplane from the ground, just as it is hard for an airplane to hit a bridge or other ground target from the air.

Dijon, France

Our winter quarters at Saint-Dizier lasted only three weeks. On October 6, we moved to Dijon. This was the first time we had been based near a large French city. Dijon was known as the Paris of the East. We stayed in an enormous chateau while there. I never understood why they built these 100-room, hotel-like structures out in the countryside. This chateau had five stories with huge columns in front, similar to an antebellum mansion in the

American South. Along the driveway leading up to the chateau were two long rows of tall, stately trees. It was a magnificent and imposing entrance. The Officers were billeted in the chateau, but the enlisted men set up tents in front of the chateau. Fall was in the air and it was already getting cold. We were about to experience Europe's coldest winter in 30 years. When we left Dijon, 28 days later, every tree had been chopped down for firewood, sacrificed to keep the enlisted warm. The chateau looked almost naked without those trees.

The airfield at Dijon was a fairly good one, except that it was short. You had to pay attention when landing. If the weather was good, it wasn't a problem, but if the weather turned nasty, you had to be careful. Late one afternoon seven P-47s assigned to the French Air Force came in to land. The weather was marginal, but they were low on gas, so they needed to land. They must have been used to a longer airfield, because the first one came in too hot and ran off the end of the runway. A moment later, a second one came in and did the same thing, ran off the runway, and then smashed into the first P-47. The third one did the same thing and, incredible as it sounds, all seven repeated the fiasco. In ten minutes time, we had seven wrecked P-47s off the end of our runway. To be fair, these pilots may not have had many hours in the aircraft and the weather was closing in fast, so they had no time to practice.

We continued to photograph many targets every day and hour we could get in the air. Some days we might only have two or three good viewing hours at a target area and there were more and more days that we couldn't get off the ground at all. Weather and flak were still our main dangers, with an occasional run from hostile aircraft. In the event of potential trouble I always climbed higher as fast as I could. With those two monster Allisons we could out climb them if we saw them soon enough.

We became acquainted with pilots from the 1st French Photo Squadron and they told us of a Swiss watch factory five miles inside the Swiss border. Since Dijon was only 100 miles from Switzerland some of us decided to pay them a visit. This was strictly illegal, though, since Switzerland was a neutral country and servicemen caught in a neutral country would be interned. As far as the US Army was concerned, if you turned up in Switzerland for any reason than being shot down, you were assumed to be a deserter. The watch factory was in a tiny mountain town, in western Switzerland. Watch making was their only industry and it looked as if the entire town worked in the watch factory.

The factory had two long, 60 foot or so, tables parallel to each other. They were completely filled with watchmakers. Each one would put in a part or two and pass it to the person on his right. By the time the watch had made it around the table, it was a finished watch. There were people who did nothing but make sure each station had plenty of the right parts. It was actually a watch assembly plant. We didn't see where the parts came from. They sold the watches to the soldiers at wholesale, so everyone bought a number of them. I sent one to my dad, my sisters Isabell and Grace, and purchased one for myself. The little factory was doing an excellent business. I am sure they were disappointed when the front and the soldiers moved on.

It was cloudy most of November, so three friends and I wangled a three-day pass to go to Paris. We stayed in a hotel at the one end of the Champs-Elysees, about a block from the Arc de Triomphe. We took the "invasion money" we had been issued when we got to France. The exchange rate against the Franc was pegged at only about one-fourth what it should have been, so Paris was going to be very expensive for us. The French people had a little money, but very few cigarettes at that time. Cigarettes became so valued they were also used as a medium of exchange. As an officer, I was issued seven packs of cigarettes per week and since I didn't smoke, I had a good supply of cigarettes. So in French eyes, I was "rich."

We went to a nightclub the first night in Paris, never asking the price of anything, and ended up with a $600.00 tab! By pooling all of our invasion money, we could just cover it.

The next day, under the Arc de Triomphe, I bartered our cigarettes for French Francs. This was frowned on by the US Army, but it was the only way we were going to be able to stay in Paris. I didn't feel guilty about it because they cleaned us out the night before. We sold our cigarettes for 100 francs per pack and we were back in business.

Saint-Nicolas (Nancy), France

As winter set in, Allied advances slowed and the front stabilized near the French-German border. That winter it started snowing in late November and there was snow on the ground until late February. With the Germans having given up southern France, we moved again, this time to a hastily constructed, temporary airfield near the village of Saint-Nicolas-de-Port (about 10 miles outside Nancy). We were to be in Saint-Nicolas only until the 3rd Army captured the airfield at Haguenau, in the upper Alsace. But the weeks dragged as the weather was bad and Allied advances minimal.

Then on December 16, the Germans launched a surprise offensive at a weak spot in the front, near Luxembourg, starting what would become a major battle in the War. That offensive was only about 75 miles north of us and the ensuing battle left us Saint-Nicolas through March 1945.

Our airfield was located on fairly smooth ground, but one end was about 30 feet higher than the other. To firm up the runway, an engineering battalion laid down a thick layer of tarpaper and over that laid a wire grid, with the wires crisscrossed in four-inch squares. These were heavy wires, about an eighth inch thick. This grid was held in place with long pegs. It was flat and smooth when they finished.

But it was flat and smooth for only a couple weeks. That winter's heavy snow and rain softened the ground and made it a difficult airfield. Getting off the ground required full throttle the full length of the runway. Landing was the opposite: once you hit the ground your roll was extremely short.

The touchdown areas at either end of the field turned into a muddy mess. It got so bad that the camera windows in the cockpit nacelles became muddied on take-off and the reconnaissance photographs were useless. This problem was quickly solved, though, by one of the camera crew. His idea was to tape a piece of paper over the camera windows with masking tape. This stayed in place through a take-off run at 100 mph, but around 200 mph the air ripped the paper off and we had clear camera windows. A simple, yet ingenious solution to a major problem.

Soon the taxiways became almost impossible to negotiate due to muddy and wet conditions. The engineers came back and filled the holes with gravel and raised the taxiways. They also reinforced and raised the revetments, the earth berms used to protect the parked airplanes. It improved the situation, but some sections of taxiway were now 18 inches above the adjacent ground. The taxiways were also narrow, so narrow that even when you were centered on the taxiway, the wheels under the engine booms were only two feet inside the abrupt taxiway edge. Naturally, from time to time, pilots accidentally taxied one wheel off the edge. This tipped the airplane alarmingly to one side as the wheel dropped from the taxiway into the adjacent mud. The wheel generally sank up to its axle and the plane was stuck. With only one taxiway, the airfield had to be shut down until the crane could pull the airplane out and back on to the taxiway.

As winter grew colder, we also faced icing problems. The brakes on the P-38 would freeze on the main wheels, so you couldn't move the planes until they were thawed.

One wet and soggy morning I taxied out from the revetment and down the muddy taxiway to the end of the runway. As I was revving up the engines preparing to take-off, a call came through to abort my take-off, the field was being closed due to worsening weather. I turned to reenter the taxiway and my right wheel moved on to a dry area on the taxiway, and the plane stopped hard. It wouldn't move even under full throttle. I shut the engines down and walked over to my crew chief to see if he could find the trouble. He soon diagnosed the trouble as a frozen brake shoe on my right wheel. My frozen wheel had skidded all the way down the muddy taxiway. I often wondered what would have happened if I had tried to take-off with that frozen wheel. I was glad I never found out. The bad winter weather had become a significant problem for us.

The best thing going for Saint-Nicolas airfield was the ease of finding it. In our sector there was a familiar canal that left the Rhine River and ran due west for about 50 miles to a railroad bridge. By turning 90° left at the railroad bridge and following the railroad south for five minutes, you could see our field from a very low altitude. This fortunate circumstance made for easy approaches in almost any weather.

If the ceiling was below 200 feet, they put rows of oil barrels on each side of the airfield and kept them lit until all the chickens were home on the roost. We flew out of that field for four months – during the worst time of the year – and never lost a plane due to weather. All the same, the sight of those burning barrels was always welcomed with a prayer of thanks.

Leo came to see me in Saint-Nicolas in mid-December.

He didn't have a pass; he just drove over from his base in the Vosges Mountains, 25 miles southwest of our airfield. General Patton's 3ʳᵈ Army had stopped their offensive there that fall and had since constructed defensive lines till the other Allied armies could catch up. At that time Leo was in the Headquarters Company of Patton's 4ᵗʰ Armored Division, where he drove a half-track (a lightly armored truck with bulldozer tracks driving from the rear and conventional wheels on the front).

Leo stayed with me in Saint-Nicolas a couple days, until the news of the German offensive on December 16. Upon hearing this, he promptly returned in case the 3ʳᵈ Army was to move to counter the German action. It was a good thing he did, because he would have been missed immediately. With Leo's own 4ᵗʰ Armored Division in the lead, the 3ʳᵈ Army was about to become one of the deciding factors in the battle that would later be known as Battle of the Bulge.

The German offensive broke through the Allied lines in the Ardennes area, near the French-Belgium-Luxembourg borders. By the time the German surprise attack became known they were already deep into the Ardennes and had surrounded an American Division in Bastogne, Belgium. Their objective was to drive to the channel port of Antwerp, split the Allied front in two and sue for a negotiated peace.

We now had a battlefront 20 miles to our east and another developing 75 miles to our north. General Patton's 3ʳᵈ Army was given the task of disengaging from the southern front, transporting his Army 100 miles north and attacking the German left flank. It was Patton's job to relieve the Division under siege in Bastogne and continue north, connecting with another Allied army driving south on the German right flank. This would create a classic pincer where the Germans would either have to pull back or risk being cut off and captured in an Allied mop-up operation.

There was a story that went through the ranks at about this time over how Patton was assigned to attack the bulge. The story related how, at an emergency meeting of Allied generals, Supreme Allied Commander Dwight Eisenhower outlined the risk and the opportunity of the German offensive. He asked each general how quickly he could move his army and attack the German flank. Supposedly the British General Bernard Montgomery said it would take him six weeks. The American General Courtney Hodges said it would take four weeks. Another general said his army needed three weeks. Then all eyes turned to General Patton. "How about it, Georgie?" Eisenhower asked.

"General," Patton supposedly responded, "say the word and I can be there in three days." And he got the job! Based on later historical accounts, this story was largely true.

To attack the German left flank, Patton's Army had to come west to Nancy to find a road suitable for his heavy armored equipment. We went into Nancy that night to watch the 3rd Army pass through. All night long the armor and troops came through: trucks, jeeps, half-tracks, tanks, 240mm howitzers, tank retrievers and command cars. It seemed like a never-ending stream.

Their route took them through the center of Nancy. There was one key corner in the city, a 90° right-hand turn that the armored caravan had to negotiate. As the early vehicles came through the turn, there was room enough for only two vehicles to pass together, but by the time the later vehicles passed this corner six vehicles could have driven through side-by-side. Fast moving armor, traveling in the dark, widened the corner by driving through and over the buildings lining either side.

What Patton had done to accomplish this bold maneuver was to leave most of his infantry in place to hold the southern front and move everything with wheels or tracks up to the bulge. Any equipment that broke down along the way was simply shoved off the road and left, nothing was allowed to slow their pace as they raced north.

To get more troops to reinforce those left back to hold the southern front while the armor was gone, a general call went out to the rear echelon units, including the Air Corps and Hospital Units, to send up ten percent of their personnel to aid the 3ʳᵈ Army. Our CO called for volunteers to go up to the southern front and he had no shortage of volunteers. Our entire mess section volunteered to the man. I guess they figured anything was better than KP.

Probably the main reason the German succeeded in surprising the Allies in their Ardennes offensive was lousy weather, which meant no photo-reconnaissance. Between November 20 and December 20, I was able to fly only three missions due to the weather; there was a two-week stretch when none of our airplanes got off the ground. The Germans were able to use that time to move 250,000 men and their equipment into place for their push into the Ardennes. Had the weather been better, our photo-reconnaissance would have caught their troop movements and our 9th Air Force would have wreaked havoc on them and probably stopped them.

It was on December 25, after 16 days of overcast, that the full force of the 9th was finally able to do what they did best, search and destroy. The next afternoon, a tank battalion from the 4th Armored Division reached Bastogne and ended the siege.

The 34th PRS was also out, over the battlefield, at first photo light that Christmas morning, photographing the entire battlefield area. We flew the pictures, complete with the intelligence reports to the waiting Field Command HQ, near Bastogne. They were dropped at low altitude to insure they were retrieved by our troops. One of our planes was shot down during this effort. This was the second plane we had lost at Saint-Nicolas. Up to that time, we had lost three flying from Chalgrove, and one each from Rennes, Chateaudun, Saint-Dizier, and Dijon. We never knew what became of any of them as we always flew missions alone. Most of the pilots were lost in one of their first ten missions. If they survived ten missions they knew pretty well what they could or couldn't do with regards to enemy fighters and anti-aircraft flak. Myself, I lived by the old adage: "He who fights and runs away, lives to fight another day." I took my time, waiting until I thought the target area was clear. This seldom took much extra time, sometimes just a different sequence of target acquisition.

Nancy was a major city and had diversions of all kinds for the young soldiers. It was also home to an Allied Replacement Depot, or "repple-depple," as we called them. New troops would pass through and be assigned to units. There was also a large field hospital in Nancy, so there were quite a few young nurses there. Not that it did us any good; I never even got to talk to one of them.

The Army took over the Nancy opera house and made it a temporary movie theater. It was a beautiful opera house, with seven balconies wrapped around the stage, all stacked up one a top the other, so every seat was ringside, so to speak. My friend, Phil Hooke, and I went to the movies one night and took along a bottle of champagne. We intended to drink it during the show. Knowing that releasing the cork would alert other servicemen to our bottle, we waited until the posse was riding after and shooting at the desperados before we worked the cork loose, hoping to mask the cork's pop with cinema gunfire. The movie was progressing nicely as we loosened the cork, but just before we released it, the movie sound quit and our "POP!" alerted the entire theater to our bottle. There were instantly twenty hands reaching from every angle. Phil and I each got one drink from the bottle and never saw it again.

There were public bathhouses in Nancy. One, like the Opera House, was quite ornate. It had a row of 24 fancy tubs, recessed in little cubicles. There were even lady attendants who would wash your back if you wanted them to. We went in to town every Saturday afternoon for a hot bath. It got to be one of the highlights of the week during that cold winter. Most of the French homes in that area did not have bathtubs at home, so the bathhouses were busy. It was quite an industry, almost like the car washes we have now.

There also was a large USO presence in Nancy. They arranged dances, provided a quiet place to write letters, served coffee and doughnuts, and did what they could to keep the soldiers contented and busy. It was a remarkable effort to provide all of this. The day after any large city was captured, the USO and the movie theatres would be up and running. All of this was at no charge for the troops. In addition to all of this free entertainment, each unit had a service officer who issued care packages every week to servicemen. These packages contained cigarettes, candy bars, razor blades and books if you wanted them. The US Army took pains to keep the troops satisfied. There was even a correspondence school that you could enroll in. I decided to take a course in medieval history, an interesting subject to me.

We had a considerable amount of time off that winter due to the weather. I saw my brother, Leo, on several occasions. Sometimes I caught rides with one of the Red Ball Express trucks.

The Red Ball Express was one of Patton's ideas to expedite freight to the front. The two best roads from the Replacement Depot and the front were commandeered and controlled for the Red Ball Express. One road was dedicated for traffic going to the front and the other for traffic coming from the front. Everything on the road moved at a designated speed or was moved off the road. The concept more than doubled the freight hauling capacity of the 3rd Army.

Because Leo was in the 4th Armored HQ Company, Patton's own regiment, I always knew where he was. Sometimes he was only ten miles from me. A few times I even walked to see him.

From these visits to see Leo, I could tell where the Germans had put up a stiff resistance. It was evident in the height of everything. The most intensive firefights cut everything off a height of about three feet. This included buildings, trees, shrubs, and anything else that had once been higher.

STORIES FROM MY YOUNGER DAYS

1945

Finishing Up and Coming Home

Saint-Nicolas, France

The Battle of the Bulge ended with Germany's retreat in January 1945. The Germans fell back and dug in at the Rhine, behind their previously prepared Siegfried Line. The battlefront became static for the first time since the breakout from Normandy.

To our south, near the Swiss border, in Alsace, the German 19th Army was being defeated in an area near Colmar, France. These German troops had fiercely defended this region since they considered it part of Germany, not France. But by early February, the German 19th Army was in retreat, trying to escape into Germany. Their only possible exit was a bridge east of Colmar, France at Breisach am Rhein. The American 1st Army, 3rd Army, and the French 1st Army were jointly closing in on the German pocket, but to trap them, the bridge at Breisach had to be destroyed.

Our Air Forces threw everything they had at that bridge. First, the fighter bombers tried, but the anti-aircraft guns were many and accurate, and the Allied losses were high, so they were pulled back with the bridge still standing. Then the medium bombers, A-20s, tried to blow the bridge up, coming in at 12,000 feet. They too were shot down with such alarming regularity that they were pulled off. Next, the heavier B-17 and B-24 bombers feet were brought in at 20,000, but they never hit the bridge. For two miles around the bridge the ground looked like craters on the moon. But the bridge remained; the bridge was the only man-made object left in the entire area.

Colmar was only about 60 miles southeast of us, so we were photographing the area six to ten times a day! I flew four missions over the bridge, running into the heaviest anti-aircraft fire I had experienced. On one of the missions, after I had taken my pictures through a heavy flak barrage, I feigned a hit and went into a spin and spun down behind a ridge of the Vosges Mountains before I pulled out, safely out of German view, and returned to base.

It was on a mission two weeks later that I almost met my maker. Some new pilots had joined our Squadron and as was our custom I took one out to fly cover with me. We took the new pilots with us to get them used to the idea that the fun and games were over and the serious flying had begun. We took off together and after we reached the target area we separated so I could photograph my targets. He was to circle while I photographed targets.

While I preparing for a run on my final two targets, the Stuttgart airfield and marshalling yards, I looked up and saw him flying straight at me from the opposite direction.

He must have seen me at the instant I saw him because we reacted simultaneously and in the same way.

We were each supposed to turn right, but neither of us did. We both dove in an attempt to fly under the airplane approaching us. We must have put the same pressure on the control column because we were then still on a collision course, though now in a 30° dive. As we realized what was happening, we each pushed the control column forward again, increasing our dive angle. Then we were in 45° dives, but still on a collision course. So again, we steepened our dives until we did pass each other. He was either stronger on his control column or perhaps his plane was rigged tighter, because he passed no more than ten feet under me when we crossed approaching 500 mph! We had started at 20,000 feet, but when we finally pulled out we were 2,500 feet above downtown Stuttgart. Besides scaring each other near to death, we had flown right into anti-aircraft hell.

We returned to base without photos of the Stuttgart targets; I figured I had got into enough trouble for one day and didn't want to push my luck further.

By mid-January, the condition of our airfield near Saint-Nicolas was so bad it was damaging the airplanes. Gravel and

Roy Teifeld in 34ᵗʰ PRS darkroom, basement of a chateau near Saint-Nicolas-de-Port, 1945. Photo courtesy of 34ᵗʰ PRS Association.

mud were flying everywhere on landings. They finally closed the field for repair. A detachment of African-American engineers arrived to repair it, filling the holes, grading it, laying down four inches of new gravel and covering it all with interlocking sheet metal. They did a bang-up job in only three days time. From that day forward we had no trouble with it. It was a noisy runway, though, making a metallic ZINGGGGGG every time we touched down.

Ground military activity slowed in February, after the German 19th Army had escaped across the Rhine. That month, I flew only six missions. The Germans were busy reinforcing their Siegfried Line and the Allied forces were bringing up fuel, food and armaments for an upcoming offensive.

Our photo and intelligence analysis, however, continued at its regular pace. In the Intelligence Trailer, we had a large map of central Europe with the battlefronts marked in grease pencil. Next to it was the Teletype machine, which linked us to the 3rd Army Intelligence and to the 10th Photo-Reconnaissance Group. The 34th PRS, like all the photo-reconnaissance units in Europe, was a part of the 10th Photo-Recon Group. Colonel Elliot Roosevelt, son of then President Franklin Roosevelt, commanded the 10th Photo-Recon Group.

The entire European Theatre was marked off in squares according to degrees, minutes and seconds of longitude and latitude. One minute of latitude equated to one nautical mile (a little more than 6,000 feet) and one second of latitude to one one-sixtieth of one minute (or roughly 100 feet). For longitude, these figures varied according to distance from the equator.

To identify ground locations precisely, the Army mapped each square mile of land into smaller squares. The smallest squares were 33 feet on a side, and were grouped in units of 25, five squares to a side. Each of these squares was named with a letter of the alphabet. This level of ground measurement, 33 foot squares, was precise enough for different units to coordinate activities and gave us a shorthand notation to quickly define a position on the radio or Teletype. A specific position could be defined using a latitude/longitude pair to identify the group of squares and the letter to identify a certain 33-foot square of ground.

Coordinates would come every morning for the new bombing targets, the Bomb Line. During this time it was my duty to keep the Intelligence Trailer map current. If the front didn't move, the mapping coordinates stayed the same. But if there were movement on the front, the coordinates would indicate it. Then the new positions would be marked on the map and the older grease pencil marks erased. You could always tell when a new offensive was planned or underway because the Bomb Line would advance several miles into enemy territory. I enjoyed keeping the map up to date. Some days the Bomb Line would advance two or three times. The old Teletype was kept busy.

That February, our A-Flight[2] was given leave to go to

---

[2] Flights are sub-groups of a squadron, typically consisting four to six pilots, crew and planes. At its largest, the 34th PRS consisted of five flights, A-Flight through E-Flight.

Paris. We received permission to fly the B-25 we kept for instrument flight practice, so this time we traveled in style. And, we were to land at Le Bourget Airport, the airport where Charles Lindbergh landed after completing his historic solo flight across the Atlantic in 1927!

This B-25 was stripped of its guns and armor. There was a nice spot in the aircraft's tail, where the rear gun turret had been, where you could lay down and get comfortable. I crawled back there and read comic books all the way to Le Bourget. By when we landed in Paris I was so airsick I could barely walk off the plane. The sway and yaw of the tail section of that plane had gotten to me. That was the only time I ever got airsick.

We stayed in Paris for a week and saw many interesting things. One of the most memorable to me was the French War Museum. It had battle flags, uniforms and weapons back to the time of Charlemagne. There had to be 1,000 suits of armor. I visited Napoleon's Tomb, which occupied a large building next to the War Museum, on the Champs-Elysees. The French saw Napoleon as a war hero. I guess it depended whose side you were on in these earlier wars.

In late February we got orders to map our sector, from the front to 50 miles inside Germany. This was an extensive area and required four full days of all out squadron effort. The Allied armies were about to mount a large offensive.

Mapping flights required flying a straight, level line over a designated ground track. We determined our course heading by adjusting for the wind speed and direction at 20,000 feet. As we flew back and forth, the relative wind would be different, changing from right to left or perhaps from a tailwind to a headwind. This

Phil Hooke and I leaving for a mission, Saint-Nicolas, 1945.

required adjusting settings on the intervalometer every time we turned around to fly the next track. Every pilot was given a 40 square mile area to map. After we completed these missions and the maps were charted, triangular gaps might show up where we made errors adjusting for the wind drift. We then had go up again and shoot photos to fill these.

The Allies attacked all along the front in early March and eventually crossed the Rhine into Germany. We were then targeting specific enemy placements, such as ammunition depots and anti-aircraft guns. We were also adding airplanes and pilots to our squadron to help keep up with the workload.

Cognac, France

Four hundred miles behind us, on the west coast of France, there were small concentrations of German forces protecting two submarine bases. In the interest of advancing toward Germany, these bases had been bypassed by the Allies. But German submarines still used the bases for staging and supplying. While the Allied losses to U-boats had been much reduced during 1944, losses were rising again since the Germans introduced their faster electric-powered submarine.

Concerned about the recently launched *schnorchel* series of U-boat, Allied headquarters wanted the bombers to take out the submarine bases at Lorient and Saint-Nazaire. But before bombers could fly, they needed photo-reconnaissance of their bombing targets and any anti-aircraft gun placements.

These bases were located on the west coast of the Brest peninsula, northwest of Nantes. This territory was assigned to the French 1st Army. The French had no photo-reconnaissance capability, so they called on the 10th PRG for help. Since our 34th PRS was already doing photo-recon work for the French 1st Army in eastern France, we got the job and I got the mission. It turned out to be a unique and memorable mission.

The mission was to be flown from the French Air Force base at Cognac. I first had to fly across France to Cognac to meet the French High Command for that area. I would receive mission instructions there. I decided that I would land at Cognac in the afternoon, brief with the French, spend the night at a hotel there, and fly the mission the following day. After the mission, I would need to return to Cognac, where the French would take the exposed film, develop and assess its adequacy. After they were satisfied that the mission was successful, I would be free to return to my base at Saint-Nicolas. The entire mission would take the better part of two days and would require me to start my engines twice without the backup battery truck and without experienced mechanics with fire extinguishers.

Otherwise, it sounded like a piece of cake and a welcomed diversion from the recent grind of mapping missions. I added some more invasion money to my wallet for dinner and a hotel room, though I had no idea how I would get to town or where I would stay.

I took off late the next morning and quickly ran into bad weather. As it was a long flight, I decided to climb above it for easier flying. I added the power and started to climb. I climbed and climbed, finally breaking out of the overcast at 27,000 feet.

I hadn't flown in this part of France so it was an interesting flight. The southwestern part of France looked a lot like California. It was big wine country, with field upon field of grapes on the south-facing hills. I guess I should have expected as much, though, as I was flying over the southern Loire Valley and into to Cognac and Bordeaux, all areas famous for their wines.

After an uneventful flight I landed at a French base outside Cognac in the mid-afternoon. It was a good military airfield, small by our standards, but functional. As I parked my plane, base personnel were already surrounding me and, judging from the stripes on some sleeves, several were high-ranking officers. I hadn't thought about it, but these soldiers would never have seen a P-38 on the ground. They crowded so close around the plane that I began to be concerned about my aircraft. The French Army quickly threw guard detail around it, so the curious were kept back from the plane.

I hadn't seen this much attention since I wrecked the P-38 showing off at Chateaudun. This time, though, it was a good deal more enjoyable, believe me. They picked me up in a '34 Ford convertible. Besides the driver, there were two French officers with stripes on their sleeves all the way to their elbows.

We loaded up and the driver sped away. The car evidently had no brakes because we never slowed down; if anyone appeared in the road the driver only honked the horn. I glanced at the speedometer we were doing 120 kph (75 mph). The closer we got to town the more the driver honked. Soon the horn was blowing almost continuously. Chickens, children, women, and anything else in the roadway ran for their lives. The driver and officers must have been used to this sort of thing, but I wasn't. We slowed down only as we reached the town square and pulled up to a hotel with enormous flourish. The driver then turned to me and gave me a big grin. I think he enjoyed the trip.

As the evening approached, we dined in the hotel. We then retired to my room, which was nice enough to make a Parisian hotelier jealous. I stowed my gear and we got down to planning tomorrow's mission. They wanted reconnaissance photographs of the bases at Saint-Nazaire and Lorient, the cities and surrounding territory, and the shoreline for 30 kilometers each direction. At 20,000, I figured it would take six runs to get it all.

After we finished planning, the French officers took me out on the town for a couple of hours. Around 8:00 p.m., they brought me back to the hotel and as they were leaving one of them turned to me and said, "I want you to know you can have anything we have in this town. And I mean anything." The offer was interesting, but I had a big mission to fly the next morning, so I declined his invitation.

The next day dawned bright and clear and I was at the airfield early to check my bird. There it sat, still surrounded by guards. The French had maintained an all night guard detail on the plane, in addition to their regular perimeter guard around the base. The attention they had given my plane and me was heart warming and I resolved to give them the very best photographs I could take.

Strato Snob, 1945.

I took off at 9:30 a.m. to begin shooting at 10:00, the optimum time for photo-reconnaissance at that time of year, offering lighting with a slight shadow for good stereoscopic images. The sky was clear all along the coast. I could begin to see my target areas by the time I reached 6,000 feet. I didn't approach the targets until I had climbed to my normal operating altitude, 20,000 feet. I decided to make the first run along the coastline. This run would give me an easy check of the wind drift, which I could then factor for the remaining runs. I planned to fly the remaining runs along north to south tracks. I flew up the coast a ways, checking it all out and determining the best position for my initial pass. I had no concern over enemy fighter aircraft; this mission was being flown 400 miles from the front, so the threat of fighters was zero.

It looked calm and peaceful below, a blue ocean stretching west, checkered green farm fields to the east, and mile after mile of white beaches forming the irregular border between them. Small villages were tucked into the rolling hills of famous vineyard land. At least the crimson tide of war had finally ebbed for this picturesque area and the people I had met in Cognac seemed so happy to be free of German occupation.

I was approaching my first photographic run and that was no time for daydreaming, though. It was not known how many anti-aircraft guns protected these bases. For all I knew, they could be asleep. No Allied forces had paid attention to the bases for seven months.

The six photo runs I had planned were all to be flown at 20,000 feet. For best results, I needed to fly these over straight ground tracks. If I encountered flak, the only variable I could change would be my speed. I decided to go in slower than normal and then increase my speed gradually through successive runs, hoping this tactic would throw their timing off and ruin their anti-aircraft aim. My last run would be made at the maximum speed I could attain without kicking in the turbochargers. This would take some fast settings on the intervalometer, but nothing I couldn't handle.

Each pass would consume about five minutes, leaving me over the target area for 30 minutes more or so. Approaching the enemy area for the first run, lined up and ready, I cut in the intervalometer and kept a good eye on my altitude and compass. Cameras rolling, engines purring and eyeballs looking.

The Germans anti-aircraft gunners weren't asleep. In fact they must have had advanced warning from radar, because they were as ready as I was. I wasn't two minutes into that first run before the sky was black with flak. It didn't seem logical that they would fire this much ammunition on one airplane. When they saw a lone P-38 overhead, they must have known what was coming next. Wouldn't they want to save their anti-aircraft shells for the bombers that would arrive in a day or two? Well, they may have had a surplus of shells, because they kept up a continuous barrage the entire 30 minutes I was over them. The sky was so black with flak and powder that I could hardly see the ground.

Needless to say, I decided not to stick to my game plan of slowly increasing my speed, I increased the throttle and propeller pitch to the max and flew each run full out. I also extended my runs farther to the north and south to give me a break between runs, hoping they would think I had finished and left the area. If anything, that may have given them more time to re-supply and reload shells, because every run was thick with flak. In struck me eerily that every one of those shells were fired only for me. I was in a mini-war of my own, 400 miles from the real war zone.

I finished the last run and hoped the photos were good ones because, despite my best efforts, the plane was seldom straight and level for very long. I doubted that I escaped without some damage, but at least everything on board still worked, as I raced back to Cognac. Back on the ground, the French counted 104 holes in my airplane. Most were small, but a few were fist-sized or bigger.

Amazingly, those that went through the wings missed the fuel tanks and fuel lines, and the holes in the ailerons missed all the control cables. And, most fortunately, the engines and cockpit were not hit. As I have already said, it is difficult to hit a small moving object in a three dimensional frame. Still, I was pretty lucky.

By 3:00 p.m., the French photo team was satisfied and I was on my way back to eastern France, arriving at Saint-Nicolas at 5:30. It had been a good day's work. That was the only time I was ever hit by anti-aircraft fire and I only got credit for a half hour of combat time.

It was our custom to buzz over our aircraft's revetment upon returning from a mission. Besides being fun, the pass alerted our ground crew that we were coming in. I usually started diving from 7,000 or 8,000 feet. This would build up my speed to close to 500 mph over the field. After which I would pull up into a high chandelle[3] to bleed off enough airspeed to make a tight turn to the field.

When the air speed indicator fell below 180 mph, I lowered the landing gear and half flaps. In addition to abruptly slowing the airplane this maneuver put it in a nose up attitude and required rapid trimming of the

---

[3] A steep climbing turn executed to slow down and change direction.

elevator. Otherwise it was almost impossible to hold the nose down. Our aircraft control surfaces (elevator, rudder and ailerons) had small tabs on their trailing edges. These tabs could be adjusted, trimmed, to relieve air pressures on the controls. Effective use of the trim tabs reduced pilot fatigue and made landings and take-offs easier.

During the War, the Army Air Corps continued a custom established in the First World War of giving each pilot four ounces of whiskey per mission. The base doctor would give us a fifth of whiskey after every seven missions.

I gave my whiskey ration to the mechanics and ground crew who serviced my airplane. They worked hard, always outside under miserable, cold and wet conditions to keep our planes combat ready. I was glad I could do a little something for them.

Haguenau, France

By the end of March, the Allied Armies had pushed east, over the Rhine and into southern Germany. In order to maintain our service efficiency we moved to Haguenau, a good-sized city in the French region of Alsace. Haguenau was 10 miles west the Rhine and about 20 miles north of Strasbourg, France.

To the east of our base, open fields sloped down to the Rhine. The Germans had fiercely defended these fields. Dead soldiers from both sides littered them. We were not allowed to remove the bodies because the area was mined. The hangars and all other buildings on the base had been blown apart and wrecked German airplanes littered the airfield, but the runway itself was concrete and in good shape. How lucky could we get?

We were assigned a local convent to live in. The Germans had used the same convent for quarters. The doors were gone, as were most of the windows, but it was close to the base and it didn't leak, so we were glad to get it. It must have housed a Gestapo office because there was a small building near the main gate full of dossiers on everyone living in the area. They had spied on just about everyone, even their own people. It wasn't long before the dossiers were strewn all over. None of us had ever seen anything like this so we were curious. Lots of the men took some home as souvenirs.

It was about this time, in April, that the Germans were firing the last of their V-2 rockets. The V-2 was their large rocket. It carried a 1,000-pound warhead. By then we were flying missions well into Germany, evidently near some of their launch sites. The first time I saw the V-2, I had no idea what it was. All I could see was that something was moving upward at a horrendous rate.

While we were over enemy territory, we were supposed to maintain radio silence unless we had something very important to say. But there were many planes in the air, all listening and transmitting on the same frequency, and the radio was actually quite busy. Most of it was serious stuff, but occasionally some of it was amusing.

Someone in our squadron must have had a near miss with a V-2 and was scared near out of his wits. While we were all out one day, we heard him come on the radio, exclaiming, "KEE-RIST, look at that P-38 go." We got a good laugh at that. After we all returned to base, though, nobody would admit to saying it.

One time, I heard a P-47 pilot on the air with a long call to his base communications section, helping them determine his position. He was lost and nearly out of fuel. After a pause, his base radio operator word came back to him: "Brown-Jug-Two, this is Ozark Base, you are 30 miles east of Munich, over." To this information, Brown-Jug-Two replied with a long sigh, an interval of silence, and a final, "Oh, shit."

We were flying missions as far across Germany as the Russian front. The Russians, like the Allies on the west, were advancing into Germany from the east. The weather was improving considerably and all the photo-recon units were busy. On April 8, our 34th PRS flew an all-time record of 42 missions in one day! By this time I had around fifty missions under my belt and was in a groove. I had flown over the same area so often that I only used a map to pinpoint target areas. Since our missions were in southern Germany, not far from Switzerland, I always returned to base by flying along the Swiss border. Then, in case of trouble from an enemy fighter or a failing engine, I wouldn't have to bailout over enemy territory. And since we usually had more film than we needed for the targets, I took many pictures of the Swiss Alps. Somehow, though, I never got home with them.

As the Germans retreated, our infantry liberated all manner of equipment. While most of it was German military equipment, not all of it was. Often it included civilian equipment, such as bicycles or cars. The soldiers that captured it didn't have time to enjoy it because they were constantly moving up to reengage the Germans. We – on the other hand, being located near the front and with free time – were in a unique position to capitalize on anything of value that the Germans had abandoned.

The first thing I "liberated" was a bicycle, the use of which extended my pilfering range and enabled Phil Hooke and I to liberate a sports car. I don't recall the make or model, but it was a classic 1930s roadster. And since we had access to plentiful aviation gas, soon every one in the A-Flight was cruising around the local countryside in a racy convertible.

During this timeframe, mid-May, while the German armed forces had surrendered, the German civilian government had not and it continued to operate. The Allied leadership had yet to assume control of Germany, so while organized, armed hostilities were effectively over, the control of Germany was still in flux.

The brother of one of our pilots stopped to visit on his way back from the front. He related how his division had captured a German airfield and flight school, complete with aircraft. The school was located just northeast of Stuttgart, only 60 miles east of Haguenau. Phil Hooke and I worked up a plan to liberate a few of the German trainers. We talked it up with the other pilots, but failed to enlist their support. We did, however, manage to get our CO's permission to go ahead with the project. He even lent us his command car and driver for the liberation.

The following morning we packed our gear and parachutes. For the promise of an acrobatic ride in a

German bi-plane, we got the mess cook to fix us a box lunch. When we got to the CO's headquarters, his car and driver were waiting for us.

This was our first opportunity to see a bombed city from the ground. It was not a pretty site; 90% of Stuttgart was little more than rubble. We did not see a single building with a roof on it. The streets were wide but so full of rubble you could barely drive through them. Outside of Stuttgart, in green hills of the Black Forest, were many smaller, picturesque villages, untouched by the War. I found all of Europe to be scenic, but this Swabian countryside had to be one of the most beautiful areas. It reminded me of my own homeland in the Pacific Northwest.

The training field we were looking for was on a mesa, 300 feet or so above the surrounding countryside, so it was not hard to locate. After a two-hour drive from Haguenau we found the field and drove through the front gate. It was incredible: not a person was there, the buildings were all intact, and breakfast was still on the mess tables. They had obviously left in a hurry.

There was the row of 25 Heinkel HE-72 trainers on the flight line. The Heinkel was a biplane, similar to the Stearman primary trainer common in America at that time. Needless to say we didn't waste any time trying to select the most suitable victims for our raiding party. We jumped out of the command car and started a quick inspection. All of the planes had a peculiar odor from the smell of their fuel. It was a synthetic gas manufactured from whatever organic material the Germans had available. We looked them over and finally settled on the two with the most fuel in their tanks. Most of the instrument panel was foreign to us, but they had compass and an airspeed indicator, so we were not too concerned. We didn't trust the gas gauges, so we measured the fuel in the tank with a stick.

We buckled on our parachutes, adjusted our goggles, since the trainers had open cockpits, strapped in and started them up. After a lengthy warm-up, we taxied past the commander's car to the runway. The Germans used a windsock just as we did to indicate wind direction. By taking off into the wind we would fly off the mesa and be at least 300 feet in the air almost as soon as we left the runway. I didn't like this too much but I figured if the Germans could do it, we could too. The driver told us that he would stick around long enough to see if we made it and if we didn't he would report it. We waved to thank him, gunned the engines and took off in formation.

The little planes leapt into the air, or it seemed so, as we left that mesa. We set a course for Haguenau and decided to fly close to the ground the ground in case any Allied fighter might decide to bag us and add to his score. The German markings didn't stand out, but they were there nonetheless.

In no time at all we were over our own field. We gave them a good buzz job, hauled up into an Immelmann[4] and set them down together in front of our flight line.

Now that these trainers were at our base, everybody wanted to fly them! These little ships flew practically all

---

[4] A half loop followed by a half roll to level, upright flight.

day long. My crew chief and his mechanics said they would do the maintenance on them, if I taught them to fly. This was too good a bargain to pass up, so I added flight instructor to my resume.

They were good students and were soon flying, though not soloing. The CO had given us strict orders that the non-pilots were not allowed to solo. Everyone had great fun with our little German

Heinkel HE-72, with me in back cockpit, May, 1945. Note the US marking we applied to the side of the fuselage.

flying school until one pilot decided to impress a friend with a loop.

With a buddy aboard, he climbed to a 1,000 feet altitude and flew up into a loop directly over the runway. The loop came out OK, if lower, but for some reason he decided to loop a second time without regaining altitude. That second loop was his last; he lacked sufficient altitude to complete it and he dove the airplane straight into the runway, killing himself and his friend.

After this accident our CO grounded our German trainers. No one flew the remaining plane again. I am sure the dead airmen's last orders were stamped "killed in action." What else could the Army say?

Shortly after this happened I drew a mission over

Czechoslovakia. I flew a different plane, one that recently had an engine replaced. Everything was fine until I got to my last target area, when the new engine started vibrating badly. I backed off on the throttle hoping it would smooth out and settle down, but it got worse. Soon the whole plane was shaking violently, so I shut the engine down. Needless to say I was more than a little glad that I was in a twin-engine aircraft. I increased the throttle on the left engine to 3,000 rpm and trimmed the ship for single engine flight. Without the trim tab to counter the tendency for the airplane to turn right, my left leg would soon have been stiff from over exertion.

I decided to forgo my last target and head home. I didn't radio the incident to Woodpile, our base radio center, because I didn't want to advertise the fact that my ship was crippled. By that time I didn't expect to see German fighters pursuing me, but I wasn't certain. I also knew that the Russians didn't appreciate Americans snooping around their front and wasn't sure what to expect from them.

Pointing the nose toward home I started a gradual descent to put me over the front at 6,000 feet. This descent would increase my single engine speed to 170 mph, which was a respectful speed under the condition. Having no trouble on the return, I eventually crossed into our territory and radioed to alert our ground crews. Under these conditions the ambulance and fire engine always waited by the runway in case the pilot had forgotten single engine landing procedures. I wasn't worried though. While I had never made a single engine landing, I had practiced the maneuver countless times. In a single engine landing the approach was made straight in, no landing pattern, the throttle on the good engine was set at full power with the flaps down to create enough lift to get into position for the letdown and landing.

Once I had started my final approach all I had to do was slowly decrease the rpm as I rolled in opposite rudder trim to counteract the diminishing pressure required to compensate for the single engine torque. There wasn't much to it. In fact, outside of the muddy conditions at Saint-Nicolas in the winter, it was the shortest landing roll I ever made, that is not counting my Chateaudun disaster.

As the War in Germany wound down, a new general was assigned to assume command of the 10th Photo Recon

Group. The general flew his own P-51 into Haguenau one day to inspect the squadrons under his command at our base.

There was, at that time, a squadron of tactical reconnaissance pilots also based at Haguenau. These pilots flew P-51s. Somewhere along the line the Photo Recon pilots worked up a little game with the Tac Recon pilots. If one of the Tac Recon boys were coming in to land their P-51s, any P-38s in the air might buzz under them on their final approach, forcing them to go around for another pass to land. If there happened to be multiple P-38s in the air, it might take the Tac Recon pilot several passes to finally get his P-51 down. Of course, the Tac Recon boys returned this favor to us when they could, so a friendly rivalry emerged.

When the new general came in to land in his P-51 there happened to be five of us up in P-38s. Each of us took a turn at spoiling his landing. By the time the general did land, he was very, very mad. We landed soon after, not knowing the trouble we were in. As soon as we were all down the general lined us up and started in on us. The sky was blue, but the language was bluer that day. After an hour or two of unfriendly advice, he told us we were through flying, he was cutting our orders for a fast return to the States and muster us out in disgrace! We didn't know what to say, but our CO eventually tired of the diatribe and came over to have his say.

He told the general that anybody who had only been in the war zone five days had no business judging tried, true and seasoned combat veterans. After giving the general his due, he turned to us and said, "Boys, no one is going back. Carry on as before, but no more of this buzzing game." This sounded like a good bargain to us, so we gave up that game that day.

This took guts because our CO was a colonel and the general obviously outranked him.

Not long after that the 9th Air Force decided to phase out P-38s, and we started to fly the P-51s as well. It took a little time to get used to them. They were much lighter and their powerful single engine generated enormous torque on take-off. One of our pilots was killed taking-off in a P-51 because he forgot to roll in the right rudder trim prior to take-off.

The Nazi armed forces surrendered on May 8, but it wasn't until May 23 that the Allies went to the civilian government's headquarters in Flensburg and arrested its members. The War in Europe was finally over.

Although we all were ecstatic that the War in Europe was over, there was still a War in the Pacific to dampen spirits a little. There was a general meeting of squadron personnel one night and a visiting general was on hand to thank us for our accomplishments and to give us an idea of what may be in store for us. He laid out the campaign that was planned for an invasion of Japan and asked for a show of hands to see how many would volunteer for this assignment. I was proud to see that every hand in our squadron went up. But this was to be at some time in the future.

For now, we gradually converted to peacetime routines at Haguenau. Before, the 34th had been a focused and coherent unit, everyone knowing their duties and getting them done. Now with little to do, dissension began to grow among the men. Before anything too radical happened, the old Army Spit-and-Polish program was instituted with two hours of daily marching drill included.

It was there that I learned what I consider the secret of a long and happy life: *Keep busy doing something.* It doesn't matter what you do with your time, just do something, hopefully something constructive.

Repatriation

A mad rush to get troops back to the States began as that summer unfolded. A point system was developed to prioritize who would be repatriated first. Points were awarded for total months of service, for overseas months of service, for battlefield citations, etc. By the mid-June, I found myself outside London, in an Army holding area, waiting for a ride home. The only way to find out when you were to head back was to read the orders posted on the base bulletin board. This was a large base and many, many orders were posted everyday, so there was always a large crowd at the board reading them. You had to wait turns to get near enough to read them.

I hoped to fly home aboard one of the C-47s, B-17s or B-24s that were returning to the states. And many guys did, but I didn't. After a month of waiting, my orders were finally posted: I would return on the *Queen Mary*, along with 14,800 other GIs.

The *Queen Mary* was the largest ship to carry troops. It made crossings in less than five days. We entrained for Scotland one evening and boarded the *Queen* in Gourock the next afternoon. As we were departing a British band gave us a rousing send off with a spirited band concert. Anyone that could get on deck was or had his head out a porthole. The upper decks towered over the dock where the band was assembled, but the lower decks were directly across from the band. After the concert was over the remaining people on the dock broke into a resounding cheer.

In the quiet moments after the cheer, with everyone feeling upbeat, someone stuck his head out of one of the portholes and shouted, "God save the Queen! We saved her the last two times." The silence was deafening. I was so embarrassed.

With almost 15,000 men on a ship designed for 2,200 passengers, things were crowded. There were four swimming pools on the *Queen Mary*, which when drained served as additional mess halls. We ate two meals a day in staggered shifts, running from 7:00 a.m. to 9:00 p.m. The ship was a monstrous, overcrowded hotel. Although no one had regular orders pertaining to any wartime duties, discipline was still needed to feed and control the troops confined in such quarters.

As an officer, by then, a first lieutenant, I was called on to find and task enough people to run the second four-hour shift at Mess Hall 5. Now there were hundreds of outfits represented on board and no organization among or between them, so maintaining discipline wasn't easy. You could tell a lower ranking soldier what to do, but there was no way to enforce your order. All I could do was ask politely, but they decided whether or not they wanted to help and a lot of them didn't want any part of it. After contacting over 100 people, I finally assembled a crew of 24 waiters. This just goes to show you that some of us – though not a lot – do like to keep busy.

The *Queen* sailed along briskly, traveling alone across the Atlantic now that the War was over. No other transports came close to her top speed of 32 knots. Despite her size, she still pitched and rolled in the swells like a smaller ship. Her bow would rise and drop 80 to 100 feet on each swell. The pitch cycle lasted around three minutes. Her roll cycle was a little longer. It was interesting to watch this movement as she tore through the North Atlantic on the sweetest ocean voyage I was ever on, returning to my native land and family.

As an officer, I had the privilege of going to the ballroom on the upper aft deck. There you could watch the ocean without chilling in the cold winds or soaking in the spray on the promenade deck. The ballroom generally had thirty to forty card games going at any time. One afternoon I saw many high-ranking officers playing cards with returning nurses. They sat at card tables placed around the ballroom, which was actually a dance floor and therefore slick. That afternoon the seas were rough, so the *Queen* was lively. As the conditions worsened, increasing the pitching and rolling, things became more interesting in the ballroom. The people standing around the ballroom walls were grabbing the handrails to steady themselves and watching the card players seated at the tables. Sure enough after a particularly high swell, the slant of the ballroom became too great and gravity took over. All the tables, all the chairs and all the card players were swept down the slanted floor to the port side. There was nothing but dust left on the ballroom floor. Fortunately nobody was hurt. But those of us standing along the rails were treated to the most humorous episode of the voyage.

At 4:00 a.m. on our fourth day out, the ship's captain announced that we were about to sight the United States of America. Everyone that could raced to an open deck and within a few minutes a long, low, dark shadow appeared in the west. There wasn't a dry eye in the bunch. Returning to our native land from the War was such an immense feeling, especially since we left not knowing if we would be coming back at all. Oh, that was a grand and glorious day, burned into my memory as no other!! Within a few hours we cruised past the Statue of Liberty

The Queen Mary enters New York Harbor, June 1945.

and up the Hudson River to our berth on 57th Street.

By this time the decks were full of discarded gas masks, canteens, extra clothes, etc. It looked as if the troops had already mustered themselves out, at least out of Army discipline. After disembarking the *Queen Mary* they sorted us out for assignment to various stateside bases. Eventually, I was put on a troop train to Fort Lewis, Washington, along with others from the Pacific Northwest.

This was not an ordinary passenger train. A temporary mess hall had been created in a boxcar at mid-train. There were eight coach cars ahead of the mess car and eight behind it. The boxcar's doors were left open, but boarded over about halfway up the opening. At meal times, troops in the front coaches passed through the mess car and continued into the back coaches behind the mess car, lining up in the back coach aisles. When the first eight coaches were empted, the men walked to their seats, filling their mess kits as they passed through the mess car. After the men in the forward coaches were served in this fashion, the men in the back coaches were served in the same, if reversed, fashion.

It was an informal ride. We stopped almost anytime we wanted. It was late July and the weather pleasantly warm throughout the six-day trip. The train's engineers were as elated as we were. They let us take turns riding with them in the main cab. If the schedule permitted they stopped for food at towns along the way so we could add variety to the dull Army diet. Before long, we tore the planks off the boxcar door and sat in the opening, legs dangling over the side, watching America pass by. After this experience I couldn't feel too sorry for bums, if they had as good a time as I was having.

There were plenty of small railroad towns in Montana,

towns with buildings on only one side of the street and railroad tracks are on the other side. We stopped at many of these and talked to the people at the stations. We were the first troop train to come through and we were always greeted with shouts of joy and happiness. In Glacier National Park the engineer stopped the train on a trestle over a lake and we went swimming. That train ride was such fun, I hated to see it end.

Two days after we pulled into Fort Lewis, the atomic bomb was dropped on Hiroshima, and two days after that, I was back in Lebanon on a thirty-day leave. A few days later, Ralph Ellensberg, a Navy man on leave, and I were swimming at the dam on the South Santiam River when we heard the mill whistle come on and stay on.

We knew what it meant: the War in Japan had finally ended. We dried off and put our uniforms on and drove into town. But by the time we arrived, a crowd had already assembled on Main Street.

People were delirious, shouting, jumping up and down, kissing each other, patting each other on the back, overjoyed at the news that the War was finally over and that our side had won. Within an hour a parade formed along Main Street. It looked like every car and truck around was full of ecstatic citizens, singing and shouting. The parade went on almost all afternoon and after the impromptu parade a street dance started. Anyone who could play music played that afternoon and into that night.

It happened that Ralph and I were the only two service men in Lebanon that day. There is no way I can describe the feelings of that day. It was too emotional to put in words. It was a privilege for me and I have always been extremely thankful that I was able to participate in that hometown celebration.

With the end of the War, rapid demobilization of the troops was expected. Already being in the States was a plus for me. After my thirty-day leave, I reported to Santa Ana Army Air Corp Base, where I started my Army life. I thought it might take a couple weeks to be mustered out, but I soon found out it was not that easy. It took two days to learn to whom I was to report.

There was nothing to do at Santa Ana. I bummed around the nearby towns, especially those along the sunny California coast. Balboa, 11 miles south of Santa Ana, was one of my favorite haunts. To anyone who grew up in the Pacific Northwest where the ocean wasn't warm enough to swim in, the California beaches were heavenly. I body-surfed, swam around the piers, sometimes swam to sailboats anchored nearby for a chat with the sailors. And while the time passed pleasantly enough, I grew impatient with the Army's hurry-up-and-wait game. September stretched into October and I had worn a groove between the bachelor officers quarters and the base bulletin board waiting for orders. Finally, on October 15, my name appeared on the board!

Two days later, I had purchased a '38 Ford sedan and was on the road to Oregon. Three more Northwest boys were mustered out along with my detachment. The four of us took off together the next day for what turned out to be a marathon drive; we drove non-stop from Santa Ana to Portland in slightly under 23 hours. This was before freeways and four-lane roads. We drove through every city's business district and traffic light along Highway 99 all the way to Portland.

I got back to Lebanon on October 18, about 5:00 p.m. Supper was being served, so I sat down to my first home cooked meal in two years. Being a civilian again was not bad.

During nearly three years in the Army Air Corps, I had acquired 580 hours of flight time, 265 hours of combat time. I had flown 63 successful missions, was awarded the Distinguished Flying Cross[5] and the Air Medal with seven Oak Leaf clusters[6]. Our 34th Photo-Reconnaissance Squadron was recognized with two Presidential Unit Citations[7]. I left the Army Air Corp with the rank of first lieutenant.

In July 1945, after I had already left, the 34th PRS relocated a final time to Furth, Germany, where it continued its photo-reconnaissance work, flying mapping to help redraw the map of Europe, including the Russian

---

[5] Per the US Army Air Corps, the Distinguished Flying Cross was awarded for heroism or extraordinary achievement in flight. The act of heroism must be above and beyond the call of duty and the extraordinary achievement must be so exceptional and outstanding as to clearly set the individual apart from his comrades.

[6] Per the US Army Air Corps, the Air Medal was awarded to recognize single acts of merit or heroism. These individuals must make a discernible contribution to operational combat. Oak Leaf clusters were used to denote subsequent awards of the Air Medal.

[7] Per the US Army Air Corps, the Presidential Unit Citation was awarded to units for extraordinary heroism in action against an armed enemy. The unit must have displayed such gallantry, determination, and esprit de corps in accomplishing its mission under extremely difficult and hazardous conditions as to set it apart and above other units participating in the same campaign. The degree of heroism required is the same as that which would warrant award of a Distinguished Flying Cross to an individual.

Me, 1945.

held territory.

The 34th Photo-Reconnaissance Squadron was officially deactivated in November 1945. Satchel charges were attached along the engine booms of its P-38s and they were destroyed.

1842325

Made in the USA